Ronnie Peterson ~SuperSwede

Ronnie Peterson
~ SuperSwede

Alan Henry
in association with Ronnie Peterson

ISBN 0 85429 175 X

First published as, *Ronnie Peterson - The Story of a Search for Perfection,* July 1975
This revised edition published November 1978

A FOULIS Motoring Book

Published by:
Haynes Publishing Group
Sparkford, Yeovil, Somerset BA22 7JJ, England

Distributed in USA by:
Haynes Publications Inc.
861 Lawrence Drive, Newbury Park, California 91320, USA

Typesetting, printing and binding Haynes Publishing Group
Editors Tim Parker and Rod Grainger
Dust jacket design Phill Jennings
Dust jacket photos Courtesy LAT

Contents

Foreword

THERE ARE SOME racing drivers who are endowed with exceptional skill. There are many who possess a high level of determination to succeed. But there are very few in world class motor racing who have the combination of these two qualities which characterise the driving of Ronnie Peterson.

Ronnie is a team manager's dream. Whatever the circuit, whatever the conditions, whether the car is achieving its optimum performance or not, Ronnie always produces an 100 per cent effort. When everything is right he makes the job look easy and when things are not quite right, his own particular combination of skill and determination provides tremendous spectator value.

He is perhaps not best known for his car-testing ability, but by quietly analysing his own driving and the equipment he is using, he quickly forms an idea of why the car is not quite right and has a very good idea how to remedy the problem. Even if his car is not as competitive as others on the track few will beat him in the race.

In recent years he has demonstrated tremendous versatility, frequently diverting his attention from Formula 1 to compete in Formula 2, sports car and saloon car events, often with great success. He always shows a great deal of enthusiasm for any new type of racing he hasn't tried before.

His popularity amongst drivers, mechanics and members of the press stems from his friendly personality and the fact he never suffers from a feeling of self-importance. His dedication to motor racing, particularly his Formula 1 racing, together with his completely professional approach should help him to win the World Drivers' Championship, a goal which he works so hard to achieve.

Alan Rees
Team Manager
UOP Shadow Racing Team

July 1975

Introduction

WHEN IT WAS FIRST mooted that I should get together with Ronnie Peterson and prepare a book about him, we were standing in the dining room of the Glen Motor Inn at Watkins Glen the evening before the 1973 United States Grand Prix. The next day Ronnie was to win the richest Grand Prix in the world. He would stride into 1974 as the man tipped as favourite for the World Championship. The preparation of this volume, we thought, couldn't have been better timed.

In retrospect, we were allowing ourselves a leeway of excess optimism. 1974 started with a glint of promise but was quickly followed by a head-long plunge into disappointment and disillusionment. If Ronnie had been driving for any other team but Lotus, he might have found himself with not a single Championship point at the end of the season. As it was, he scored three Grand Prix victories in his faithful old Lotus 72, so it's a measure of his and his team's calibre when they can reflect on 1974 as a highly disappointing year. It was decided to postpone the book for a few months, but a reappraisal of the situation at the end of the year made it clear that we'd be guilty of a major sin of omission if we left the project incomplete. Champion or not, Ronnie has earned himself the undisputed reputation as the fastest racing driver of his era.

This, then, is the story of 'SuperSwede'; of his racing, his ambitions and his background. Any biography tends to be coloured by the personal feelings of the person who writes it; I have to confess myself as an unashamed Peterson fan. In a colourful and highly exciting world, he is a king pin, a man whom all his rivals fear. He may not be World Champion yet, indeed he may never grasp that exclusive tag, but already he has achieved the distinction equalled only by men such as Stirling Moss, Jim Clark, Jochen Rindt and Jackie Stewart. Although not yet a Champion, he is a yardstick, the man by whose performances others measure whether or not they are 'in the same race'. His Grand Prix tally is still in single figures, but his practice times are invariably a barometer by which others assess their lap times. He is a supreme competitor and he knows but one way to drive; flat out!

There are many people who have helped, both wittingly and unwittingly, in the preparation of this book. Specifically I must gratefully thank Colin Chapman, Alan Rees and Robin Herd for giving up valuable time to speak into a tape recorder; Brian Hart for long hours spent round dinner tables dissecting Ronnie's achievements; to Peter Warr and Max Mosley for some fascinating background details and off-the-cuff comments about their drivers over the past couple of years. My colleagues Mike Cotton, John Teague and Murray Taylor at *Motoring News* offered encouragement at the right times and many of the photographs between these covers are the work of Michael Tee, Laurie Morton and John Dunbar, all LAT photographers. The collections of David Winter, Mike Keppel and Jutta Fausel and Ronnie's personal scrapbook have been raided to provide others. Finally I must acknowledge the effort of my wife Carole who still married me despite the flood of typing I persuaded her to do during her lunch hours while we were engaged. Most of all, thanks must go to Ronnie and Barbro for the help and encouragement they have offered.

Alan Henry
Daytona Beach
February 1975

Over five years have passed since Ronnie and I agreed to collaborate in preparing this book about his career: and it's over three years since we produced the volume at the 1975 British Grand Prix, when Ronnie's career was probably at its lowest ebb.

The mixed fortunes that he experienced throughout 1976 and '77 made it difficult to see when we would ever be able to get together and update this work. Only in 1978 did we speak again about adding to his life story. We agreed that we would update it to the end of the '78 season, and Ronnie joked, "We can always do it again when I win the Championship in 1979." Sadly, there will be no further additions to the Peterson story. I don't propose to add to the tributes that have been paid to him except to say that it still seems totally incomprehensible that we've seen the last of this genuine and popular man. I shall always be happy that I had the chance to write this book and I'd like to think that it goes some small way towards keeping fresh Ronnie's memory.

Alan Henry
November, 1978

Photo credits
Ronnie Peterson collection: *pages 14, 18, 19, 20*
Jeff Bloxham: *page 70*
Jutta Fausel: *pages 85, 87*
David Winter: *pages 25, 39, 40, 41, 58, 59, 68, 73, 77, 78, 79, 81, 82, 83, 86*
Michael Keppel: *pages 23, 27, 35, 51, 89 bottom, 93, 100, 103, 105, 106, 112, 117, 126, 129, 131, 134, 138, 144, 150, 153, 162, 189, 190/191, 192, 193,*
LAT photographers: *pages 7, 34, 37, 38, 43, 44, 48, 55, 57, 63, 65, 89 top, 91, 94, 109, 114, 120, 122, 123, 133, 141, 146, 151, 155, 160, 163, 165, 167, 169, 171, 174, 176, 178, 179, 181, 188*

CHAPTER 1
The blond boy
from Orebro

WHEN YOU LEAVE Stockholm and head for the north west, driving up past the shores of Lake Mälar, one of Sweden's 96,000 or so natural lakes, following a path through Södertalje and Eskilstuna and keeping going for about 130 kilometres, you'll arrive at the end of Lake Hjälmar. You'll by now be well into the East Swedish Midlands, historically an area which nurtured the early Swedish state and now has the highest intensity of population of the whole country. Around 2.8 million people - about 35 per cent of the Swedish population - live and work in an area of about 44,000 square miles against a backcloth of plains separated from each other by heavily forested and strikingly colourful hills.

Sweden's East Midlands is made up of the country's capital city, Stockholm, and the five provinces (rather like counties) of Uppland, Västmanland and Närke, Södermanland and Östergötland. At the western end of Lake Hjälmar you'll find the busy, medium sized town of Örebro with its population of around 90,000 people. Many years ago, the cattle breeders of Smaland used to come up to the Bergslagen area to exchange their hides for metal goods and utensils. Not surprisingly, Örebro quickly gained a reputation as the 'shoes town' specialising in all manner of footwear. Half the footwear made in Sweden came from this area.

Örebro's main connection with fast moving wheels, at least up until the start of the 1970s, was confined to Swedish railway system which has its main workshops situated in the town in addition to its central marshalling yards. On a more thoughtful note, Sweden's new national prison is only 14 miles away from the town centre.

Otherwise, Örebro is much as any solid, middle class Swedish town could be expected to be. In fact, much like any solid middle class town anywhere in half a dozen European countries. More particularly as far as this tale is concerned, it is the home of a particular Peterson family, a surname which many families all over Sweden have been left with. This particular family owned a comfortable prosperous bakery business in the years before the Second World War, but that generation's son Bengt grew up with a fascination for things mechanical. Motorcycles and motor cars proved compelling sources of endless interest and, rather than follow his parents' foot-

Ronnie's father Bengt Peterson, the source of much encouragement and guidance in the early years with the Robardie Karts and Svebe Formula 3 car

steps into the bakery business, Bengt chose to take an engineering apprenticeship.

Bengt's mother, who had run the business since the death of his father before the war, herself sadly died just after the end of hostilities, almost at the point when Bengt was poised to take his final qualifying examinations. Faced with the difficulties of getting a job, Bengt decided to abandon engineering studies and throw his lot into the family bakery business. It must have been a hard decision. But Bengt had married a few years earlier and had responsibilities which had to be taken seriously. On 14th February 1944, his wife May-Britt, gave birth to the first of two sons. They christened the baby Bengt-Ronnie and it was he who was destined to bring a degree of fame to Örebro which all the shoes and railway engines in Sweden could never do.

Whilst Bengt and his mother looked after the pastry requirements of Orebro, not only making and selling his own fresh bread and cakes but also delivering them to a vast number of other shops in the town, Bengt-Ronnie grew up alongside his young brother Tommy who arrived on the scene in 1946. Even before he went to school for the first time, Ronnie, (as the eldest was universally now referred to), had been taken along to visit his first motor race. His father retained his interest in mechanical matters and had built a 500cc Formula 3 car which he raced under the floodlights at the local dirt track stadium. There was no international racing in Sweden then. In fact the first permanent circuit in Sweden at Karlskoga, a few miles from Ronnie's Orebro home had yet to be born.

There's every reason to suggest that Ronnie, a rather quiet and retiring child, wasn't the least bit interested in his father's motor racing activities. Probably he was too young to understand what was going on; Bengt Peterson finally stopped driving before his eldest son was six years old. Anyway, from the age of seven, Ronnie Peterson had a lot more to occupy his time for that's the age at which full-time schooling starts for Swedish children.

Not surprisingly speedway grew fashionable in the 1950s, very fashionable indeed, and it didn't take a great deal of imagination on Ronnie's part to see the possibilities offered by his and his friends' pedal bikes. They'd not been attending school very long before they'd mapped out an impromptu circuit in the school garden where they spent most of their time crashing around in the dust and dirt, allegedly learning the rudiments of two-wheeled control.

Unfortunately motorcycling wasn't on the curriculum on Ronnie's school - at least, not for the under ten year olds! Inevitably he and his friends were forced into more conventional outlets for their enthusiasm, such as football. Ronnie hated football.

"They got really upset with me for crashing round on my bike" Ronnie recalls almost mournfully "and I got very cross and upset with them

15

when they tried to make me play football. I'd just walk after the ball and that used to get the masters even more annoyed. So they thought 'he's obviously no good out in the field, so we'll put him in goal'. So they put me in goal which I HATED. I just had to stand there taking all the knocks from the ball". Somehow, I can sympathise with the masters a little. Persuading Ronnie to do something he's against was extremely difficult. He's had another twenty years' practice since then as well!

Somehow, despite this reluctance, Ronnie found his way into the school team on occasions "but I was always being forced to do that" and he also took part in handball, ice hockey and "something we call bren ball. You throw the ball and hit it with a bat. Rather like baseball". It's strange for a man who later displays such a degree of ice-cool, accurate judgement and lightning reflexes behind the wheel of a 180 mph Grand Prix car that Ronnie always hated ball games on the grounds that he could never judge where the ball was going.

"I never had an eye for the ball" he admits "I was always interested in running and jumping and was quite good at the high jump and long jump - that's probably why I liked it. I've played squash and tennis quite often since I've lived in England, but I always feel that the bloody ball is tricking me, it never seems to come where I think it should come". As an afterthought he adds "Golf isn't too bad, but squash ... I find that very tricky indeed".

In the classroom, the young Peterson admits to being a naughty little child like anyone else. He didn't have any favourite subject although when he took time off from fighting his younger brother Tommy, he did generate a bit of a liking for natural history. But he hated English and once got into a heated row with one of the teachers about why he was being forced to learn it. "I hate it" Ronnie argued "Why should I learn it. I'm never going to go to England". In 1971 Ronnie moved to England, admitting "I didn't understand a word when I first came here". After spending eight years being educated, Ronnie Peterson left school at the age of sixteen, shrugging aside the opportunity of going on to university. Other matters, more important to him, were occupying all his available time.

Back in 1952 English motoring magazines were enthusing over the achievements of a young Surrey lad called Mike Hawthorn whose driving of a Cooper-Bristol definitely marked him out as something rather special in the motor racing world. In far away Sweden, a little boy who was later to command just as many column inches as Hawthorn ever did, actually came to own his first motor car. Ronnie's ingenious father built him what amounted to a pedal car fitted with a 50cc engine. Later this grew to 125cc and the country lanes round the Peterson family's cottage soon echoed to the scream of Sweden's greatest racing driver, learning the basics of his business at the early age of eight.

Don't be fooled by that baby faced outlook. If anyone ever thinks that Ronnie Peterson lacks push when it comes to business matters, then they are making a great error of judgement. It didn't take long for this speed-happy toddler to lay out a circuit, and a timing line and organise competitions amongst his friends. Whenever Peterson and his friends had a few days off from school, they'd all cycle out to the country cottage and stage non-stop racing programmes. When they'd finished crashing round in their little cars during the day, they then graduated to practising for Le Mans by racing their cycles at night. Even at this early stage, there didn't seem much doubt what Ronnie Peterson wanted to do with his life.

It was a short step from the 'kiddy car' to full-scale scrambling and at the age of sixteen, Ronnie acquired a 50cc scrambles motorbike. He did quite well in his first year, only for the bike to be stolen just as he was planning to exchange it for a new 250cc model for the following year. He asked his father to lend him some money to get back into action, but Bengt wasn't terribly keen on his son's activities and refused to step in with financial aid. By this time the lucky owners of Renault cars in the Örebro area were fortunate enough to be having their cars serviced by the fastest Grand Prix driver in the world. He was working as a fitter in the local Renault distributorship, using every penny he earned to finance his motor-cycling activities.

Then came the productive point of contact between father and son as far as Ronnie's racing plans were concerned. Ronnie decided that he would move into karting, so he actually started to build up his first machine from some motorcycle parts. Bengt, thinking back to those happy days when he raced Formula 3 immediately after the war, grew very interested in his son's project. It didn't take the enterprising Ronnie much longer to convince his father that he really ought to help in building up the kart, so the partner-ship was forged. Bengt and Bengt-Ronnie started to build up their first kart at the end of 1961.

The first engine they used was a German 200cc Ardie motor and his father and son team christened their creation the 'Robardie' after Ronnie, Bengt and Ardie. At the age of 18, in February 1962, Ronnie Peterson took part in his very first proper race on four wheels. At that time there were several kart tracks dotted around all over Sweden. Ronnie's first race was at Höhe in Southern Sweden, but he went on to compete with the Robardie at Laxa, Malmö and Gothenburg. But all these were merely 'regional' events and there remained just a single race which counted for the Swedish Cham-pionship. And the blond boy from Örebro finished second in that event behind Ingvar Nilsson. After that year Nilsson stopped racing, so Ronnie acquired his Bultaco engine to power his own machine. Ronnie's father designed a brand new kart to accept his newly acquired engine and this was much quicker than the original Robardie. It used aluminium in the main, but also sophisticated ingredients such as titanium. It even had camber on the rear wheels. Ronnie was very proud.

Chasing round the straw bales pursued by 1965 European Kart Champion Guido Sala (No 1).

In 1963 Ronnie won the Swedish Championship with the Bultaco powered kart - in fact he won just about every race in which he took part. But by the end of the year, competition was hotting up and interest in kart racing had really snowballed. So Bengt and Ronnie made even more modifications to the kart, adding such refinements as magnesium wheels and disc brakes. The kart became highly technical and very expensive, it was however a fabulous year for Ronnie Peterson as he won many races.

Success on native soil prompted Ronnie and his father to look further afield for 1964. Having mainly concentrated in national 250cc events, they decided that they would move into the international arena in

1964, competing in Class A, for 100cc machines using no clutch or gears. It turned out to be very much an exploratory season and the Swedish hero finished 'about 13th' in the European Championship. For 1965 he refined the kart even further and started to win almost every major race he entered in, moving up to third place in the European Championship which was won by petite Italian girl Suzy Raganelli.

Ronnie had already learnt the meaning of 'oversteer' at this early stage in his career

In 1966, Ronnie, who was by now working as a lift installation engineer - an historical nicety which makes his Formula 1 mechanics' blood run cold - reached the pinnacle of his karting success. He triumphed in the European Championship and went to the final of the World Championship at Copenhagen confident that he could snatch that title as well. Once more he was facing Suzy Raganelli, in fact the Italian girl was the only other kartist who could stop Ronnie from winning. All over the weekend Ronnie's engine seemed to misfire so he and his father kept changing engines to see if they could get to the root of the problem. But still the engine misfired and Ronnie found himself beaten in the World Championship by a girl. Later they discovered that the carburettor float chamber was cracked, and as they had always tacked the same carburettor onto the fresh engines, they didn't find out what was wrong until after the event.

This major disappointment certainly didn't deter either Ronnie or his father; in fact Bengt was by this stage keener than ever to build his own **19** racing car. Ronnie wanted to move into single seater racing cars, but before he could obtain a licence he was obliged to go through a course of instruction at the Karlskoga racing circuit. Basically he had to drive a few laps of the circuit accompanied by an instructor "learning the line and all that rubbish" as Ronnie scornfully remarked.

Bengt lent his son his precious Mercedes-Benz for the test, confident that Ronnie wouldn't be foolish enough to write off the family transport (at this early stage in his career). When he arrived at the school at Karskoga he was introduced to his instructor, the man who would accompany him round the track in the Mercedes. His name was Reine Wisell.

The saga of Ronnie and Reine had begun. It was a saga which would eventually earn them a reputation as the two fastest Formula 3 drivers in Europe during 1968 and 1969. They were two very different personalities but they both looked distinctively Swedish with pure blond hair and good looking features. Reine was slightly older than Ronnie and his Formula 3 career earned him a reputation as a smooth stylish driver while Ronnie was to be known as the 'wild man' of Formula 3. The culmination of their 'competition' was to be at Monte Carlo in 1969 and some go so far as to say that Reine was never quite as quick after being beaten fair and square by Ronnie under the gaze of the Grand Prix teams. Even at the time this book is being prepared, racing enthusiasts all over Europe still remember that particular race as probably the greatest event in the history of the 1-litre Formula 3. Certainly, it was the most significant.

In action with the Formula 3 Svebe. "It wasn't as good as a Brabham and cost twice as much" is Ronnie's verdict on his first proper single seater

Reine eventually graduated to the works Lotus team at the end of 1970, but he stayed only a year. Colin Chapman replaced him at the end of 1971 with Dave Walker and then Reine drove some races as a BRM team member. Reine was never as quick as Ronnie, that's for sure, but he often suggested in the Swedish press that the reason Ronnie was so fast was that Colin Chapman gave him better cars. Certainly the type 72 was better in 1973 than it had been in 1971, but Reine was seldom as fast as Fittipaldi and Ronnie eventually turned out faster than him as well!

Back at Karlskoga in 1966, Reine and Ronnie hardly knew each other. Reine had started racing saloon cars in 1965, but because of the small racing calendar in Sweden, had gained appreciably less circuit experience than Peterson had during his karting days. Reine could race saloons only five or six times each year, whilst Ronnie's karting programme included upwards of 35 events.

Reine didn't take life too seriously in those days. But he knew full-well that Ronnie Peterson wasn't just any old driver chancing his luck. He was sufficiently perceptive to appreciate how good Ronnie was. It was only a formality for Ronnie to get through the test and, later the same day, he took part in a Formula 3 race in one of the school cars. It was only a race between school pupils, but Ronnie Peterson won. As he said much later, you could say that Reine taught him rather well!

The decision was taken. Ronnie and his father would build up a

RONNIE PETERSON

Formula 3 car, a neat spaceframe copy of a Brabham which was to be called the Svebe but which proved to cost about twice as much in the long run as it ever would have done had they bought a Brabham in the first place. But Ronnie was started on the long road to success and, all through the summer of 1966 he campaigned the Svebe in local Formula 3 races in Sweden and Denmark. He raced on the Falkenberg road circuit, chased round the straw bales at Skarpnack airfield and raced on the permanent circuits at Knutstorp, Bengtsfors, Mantorp Park, Kinnekulle and Karlskoga. Having to work during the week meant that he and his mechanic were forced to drive home to Orebro in the Volkswagen pick-up truck all through the Sunday night after the race if they ventured as far afield as Denmark. This remorseless self-denial came to a head one night when the mechanic fell asleep whilst driving and the next thing Ronnie knew was that he was sitting in the middle of the road with gear ratios, tyres and wheels scattered all round him. They'd run end-on into the side of a bridge and emptied the entire contents of the little pick-up all over the road for about a hundred yards in every direction!

At the end of 1966, Ronnie decided to buy a secondhand Brabham. The Svebe had been alright for him to learn with, but suspension designs were being updated every year and it really proved necessary for him to have a slightly newer chassis if he was to have much chance of improving. So he bought a Brabham BT18 from German driver Kurt Ahrens and used that throughout 1967.

Though he didn't realise it, in 1967 he was to have his first contact with a man who later influenced his career to a great extent. The place was Keimola in Finland, the occasion was a combined Formula 2/Formula 3 International meeting and the man was Alan Rees. Just six top line Formula 2 cars headed the field as a result of a special deal arranged by Winkelmann Racing star Jochen Rindt and his father-in-law Curt Lincoln, a wealthy individual who held a great deal of sway in Finnish motor racing circles. Jochen had married Lincoln's beautiful blond daughter Nina and the hard-headed Austrian turned his business brain to arranging an attractive financial arrangement for himself, Jim Clark, Graham Hill, Jack Brabham, Frank Gardner and Alan Rees. Glancing through the entry list, Rees noticed that Peterson's name was paired against an old Brabham BT15. And he'd gone very quickly in practice. Rees filed that knowledge into the back of his memory and didn't think anymore about it.

Ronnie Peterson's baptism into international racing was just a little bit hectic. He qualified 15th on the grid for a race at Karlskoga to which several British based teams had been invited at the end of 1966. The cars to beat in Formula 3 at the time were the Chequered Flag Brabham of Chris Irwin and the Charles Lucas Lotus 41s of Piers Courage and Roy Pike. Ronnie was racing with one of the local competitors when Pike came up to lap him. Suitably impressed, Ronnie moved to one side to let Pike through only for the American to push Ronnie into the ditch as they drove smoothly

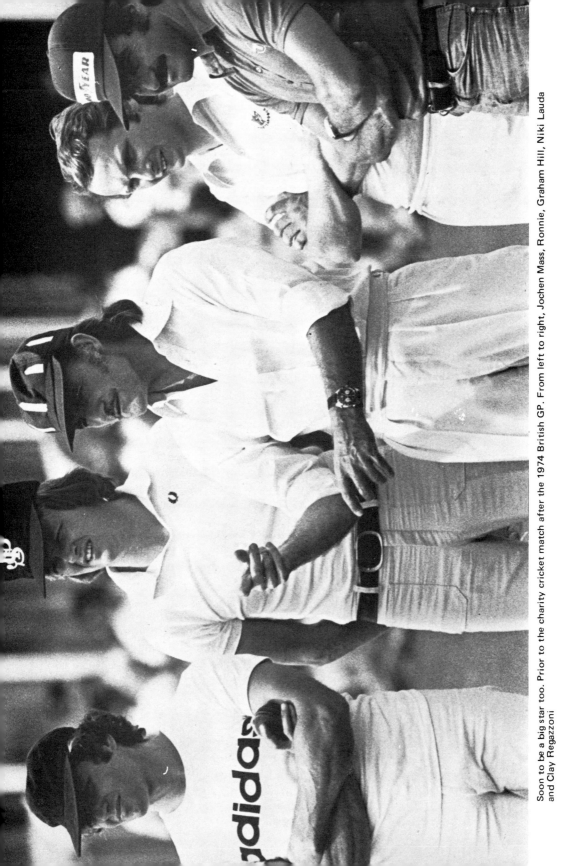

Soon to be a big star too. Prior to the charity cricket match after the 1974 British GP. From left to right, Jochen Mass, Ronnie, Graham Hill, Niki Lauda and Clay Regazzoni

out of the corner.

I wonder, thought Ronnie, as he bounced along the ditch and then fishtailed back onto the track, can this sort of thing be normal? After the race he wanted to go and tell Pike he was a bastard but thought twice and realised there wouldn't be much point. Ronnie couldn't speak any English. It was one of the few occasions he wished he'd listened a little more attentively to his English master.

Throughout 1967 Ronnie raced the Brabham on much the same basis as he'd driven the Svebe, taking part in all the local Scandinavian races plus as many internationals as he could manage. But he wasn't really making anything of it. He could scrape home with thirds, fourths and fifths in local races, but he wasn't even getting near the front of the grid for the international events.

Depression set in. He trailed all the way down to Villa Real in Portugal to compete in his first international race outside Sweden only to take one of his Brabham's wheels off against a kerb stone during practice. Very carefully he borrowed a pop-rivet gun from a fellow competitor and painstakingly riveted the broken upright together. It lasted just long enough for Ronnie to complete three laps, collect his starting money and pay his way back to Sweden.

Then he decided to try his hand at Brands Hatch, joining fellow Swedes Freddy Kottulinsky and Ulf Svensson on a ferry for England only to have rough seas delay their arrival by over twenty hours. That meant they all missed practice and were obliged to start their heats from the back of the grid after three untimed laps. Ronnie had never seen Brands Hatch before, so it's not surprising that he felt pretty depressed and failed to qualify for the final.

What should he do for 1968? He had very little money and there was only a slim chance that the Brabham would be sufficiently competitive in 1968. Talking to Reine Wisell, he heard that his fellow Swede was about to go down to Bologna in Italy to take delivery of a brand new Formula 3 car called a Tecno. Now Ronnie had heard a lot about Tecno. They were responsible for building some of the very best karts around when Ronnie was competing in the European Championship with his Robardie. And he'd also heard, along with Reine, about the way in which Clay Regazzoni had beaten all the regular Formula 3 opposition at Madrid's Jarama circuit at the end of 1967. Clearly, thought Peterson, this merits some thought.

After discussions with his father, he approached the local bank manager for a personal loan. There seems to be some doubt as to whether the bank manager ever precisely understood the nature of the goods which were to be acquired with this money - history relates that Ronnie skirted round the precise purpose with tales of "a house ... or something". Well, the "or something" turned out to be a brand new Tecno Formula 3 car which Ronnie picked up from Bologna at the same time as Reine collected his car.

A lurid moment at Karlskoga with Ronnie's first Formula 3 Tecno. A front stub axle has broken, leaving Peterson with braking on the rear wheels only

RONNIE PETERSON

The two Swedish 'coming men' travelled down to Italy together.

There were no fewer than sixty five international Formula 3 races dotted all over the Continent in 1968. This world of highly tuned 1-litre Ford engines was the accepted hunting ground for the aspiring Grand Prix star of the future and was closely followed by astute Formula 1 team managers. Equally, for the impecunious enthusiast on a shoe-string, there was a sufficient number of races all over Europe in which to avoid the top stars and collect some money. You didn't have to race against the leading lights if you trailed your Volkswagen pick-up truck carrying your old Brabham to Roskilde in Denmark, to Vallelunga in Italy, to Brno in Czechoslovakia or to Opatija in Yugoslavia.

Reine Wisell started the season with a bang. He won races at Jarama and Barcelona, came second to Roy Pike's Titan at Pau in South West France and then headed north for home and the Anderstorp International which he won from Trevor Blokdyk's Titan and Ulf Svensson's Brabham. Ronnie started more slowly. He came fourth in a Monza slipstreamer in April, beating Reine into fifth place. But this was a 'slipstreamer special', won by that arch-expert of this craft, Jean-Pierre Jaussaud. Neither Ronnie nor Reine really knew what on earth they were doing, blinding flat-out round Monza with cars on all sides of them.

Still, Ronnie had learnt enough about the ways of Formula 3 to win a race at Hockenheim later in the year by a whisker from his old friend Freddy Kottulinsky. It was going to be a long race, over 100 miles, and Ronnie realised he was going to run short on fuel if he wasn't careful. So he and his mechanic enterprisingly devised a system to carry extra fuel in what was supposed to be the oil catch tank. Even this ploy would only just get them the distance but the scrutineers turned this down when they inspected the car before the race, so he conspired with Kottulinsky in a scheme to take both of them ahead of the local opposition.

The deal was that Freddy would 'tow' Ronnie away from the opposition in his slipstream, thus ensuring that Ronnie's Tecno would run as economically as possible and they would both get clear of the field as quickly as possible. Freddy agreed that this would be fine and away they went. At least he thought it was fine until Ronnie, riding steadily behind him to the last corner, dived out of his slipstream and won the race by a length!

Freddy wasn't in the least amused at the time, but Ronnie escaped up to Hammeenlinna in Finland where he was trounced by local rally ace Leo Kinnunen in a Titan Mk 3A. That helped to achieve him a sense of proportion after fooling his friend, but he beat Svensson at Skarpnack and gained the pinnacle of his ambition by leading a Tecno 1-2 at Hammeenlinna again later in the year, beating Reine back into second place. One more win topped his successful year and that was at Monza where he beat Ulf Svensson once more.

Although it had been a successful season, Ronnie Peterson was still

Studying Barbro's table tennis technique, Kyalami Ranch 1975

little known outside Scandinavia. By contrast Reine Wisell's policy of competing in the bigger international races not only added to his store of experience, it also raised him in the estimation of talent spotting constructors. As a direct result of his efforts with the Tecno, Reine was invited to drive the works Chevron B15 Formula 3 car for British constructor Derek Bennett.

The magazines' reviews at the time raved about Reine. *Autosport's* Ian Titchmarsh summed up in that magazine's annual review that "The outstanding driver of 1968 must be Reine Wisell, the Swedish driver who showed ever-increasing promise in obsolescent machinery for the past two years, went down to Italy and bought himself a Tecno. Whenever he raced Wisell was a force to be reckoned with, even on a completely strange circuit where skill rather than slipstreaming ability counted ...". As far as Bengt-Ronnie was concerned, he was dismissed as "another Swede who changed a Brabham for a Tecno" and won the Swedish Championship. But the one chink of light is the acknowledgement that "this former kart champion may have more flair, if less dedication, than his compatriot".

He certainly proved to have more flair than his compatriot, but he wasn't short on dedication either. Ronnie Peterson's successful achievement in winning the Swedish Formula 3 Championship whilst Wisell was primarily occupied racing outside Scandinavia paid off at the start of 1969. Ronnie rustled up an agreement to run with backing from SMOG, the Swedish division of the Richardson and Merrell cough drops firm, and he went straight back to the little Tecno factory where he ordered a brand new machine for 1969. An agreement with Novamotor, the successful Italian tuners of Ford 1-litre Formula 3 engines, ensured that he would have the best power units that money could buy. This was to be the season in which Ronnie Peterson made his name.

Ronnie began his association with Tecno long before I joined *Motoring News* in 1970 at a time when I spent my spare time writing freelance race reports for the paper. Formula 3 was the pinnacle for me, and if I ever got the chance to actually write about it, as far as I was concerned, that was more important than a Grand Prix. I mention this only to remind enthusiasts in 1975 just how much attention was focused on the 1-litre Formula 3. It proved some of the most exciting spectacular and highly dangerous racing I have ever seen and proved largely responsible for developing the talents of Emerson Fittipaldi, Tim Schenken, Howden Ganley, Jean-Pierre Beltoise in addition to Ronnie himself.

Success depended on a great number of factors being exactly right. One had to have the right tyres, right gear ratios and the right chassis. And these were only basic requirements. From that point on you were obliged to drive right on the limit, flat out, all the way for all of the time. A missed gear change, an incorrect line on a corner, and a dozen cars had slipped by. There was no room for the half-hearted in top class Formula 3.

Ronnie says that he likes to drive smoothly and develop a 'tram line' technique. His track record tends to suggest that this just isn't the case, for the early 'tail-out' style which developed from his karting days blossomed out when he drove the Tecno in Formula 3. Coming from a kart manufacturer, not only was the Tecno primarily an oversteering car, but it could also be held at some quite ridiculous angles for absurdly long periods of time. All the way through his career, Ronnie's cars have oversteered. Right up to his Grand Prix cars of 1975. Oversteer is as much a trademark of Peterson's driving style as red paintwork is the trademark of any Italian racing team. It's always been that way.

He learnt to be a thinking driver in Formula 3 as well. Having worked out how to fox people like Kottulinsky at Hockenheim, he also kept an eye out on the Monza organisers who seemed keen on depriving him of a victory so as to enable a local driver to win the race. He noticed that the official at the start line just happened to hang out the 'LAST LAP' sign one lap too early with the intention of forcing Ronnie to lead into the last lap proper and then be passed by his rival. He kept an eye on the other Tecno, hung back and won.

Ronnie's second year with Tecno in Formula 3 also earned him the Swedish Championship and a degree of acclaim in his home country. The small Volkswagen pick up truck was swapped for a larger Mercedes-Benz van. He even managed to pay off his loan to the local bank. Life was becoming just a little more comfortable as Ronnie Peterson steadily moved up the rungs of the ladder of racing success.

Shortly before he drove his first race for Alan Rees, Ronnie made the acquaintance of somebody who was to have a profound personal effect on his life in the years that followed. A tall, slim natural blonde girl caught his eye in an Orebro discotheque one evening. Her name was Barbro Edvardsson, a gentle 21-year old with a flashing smile which seemed to light up the whole of her face. Ronnie, although he'd be the last to admit it, was smitten. They've been together ever since and at the end of April 1975 became Mr and Mrs Ronnie Peterson.

The greatest believer in Ronnie's ability to become World Champion, Barbro's great strength to her man has been an utter and complete devotion and support for any decision he takes. Not pushy or obtrusive like some of her contemporaries, but completely feminine, she admits that it's not for her to try and influence Ronnie in any decisions he might make.

"I believe it is not for me to make a great fuss" she explains in her delightful Swedish accent "Ronnie has enough to think about without me making great emotional scenes. Obviously I sometimes wonder to myself about things which affect Ronnie, but I think a woman should keep her emotions to herself". She paused for a moment and added "But I admit that can be difficult sometimes".

Since 1971 their home has been England and in 1973 they moved into a tastefully decorated Georgian style detached house in a fashionable area of Maidenhead. Inside it's strikingly furnished with a soft leather three piece suite in the living room, a wall to wall carpet in pale gold under foot marred only by a dark patch where Ronnie spilt a whole bottle of red wine a couple of winters ago. It's the sort of place that one would expect to find a successful stockbroker or barrister living. The neighbours are as politely unobtrusive as Ronnie and Barbro have always been. Many of them probably don't even realise that the blond youngster with the silver BMW 532 who lives across the road, the quiet Swede with a passion for collecting tropical fish, is the world's fastest racing driver. And Ronnie isn't about to walk over and tell them either.

CHAPTER 2
Three year March

MONACO HAS BEEN the high spot of the European motor racing season for almost half a century. Its unique combination of the shimmering Mediterranean, millionaires' yachts lolling on its sleepy surface, and the towering architectural backcloth of apartment blocks and five star hotels combine to provide a magnetism which captivates young and old alike. For the wealthy it provides a haven of tranquility for much of the year, for the man in the street on his package tour it is an intrusion into a way of life he's previously only read about.

For the racing driver it means something else. With up to nineteen gear changes to the lap, unyielding kerbs ready to inflict mortal damage on errant wheels and, often as not, a searing spring sun overhead, the streets of Monte Carlo provide a vicious challenge to car preparation and driver concentration. Those who master Monaco's intricacies are true sporting stars, and a glance back over the race's record book supports this supposition with names like Nuvolari, Chiron, Fangio, Moss, Hill and Stewart amongst their number.

In fact, 1969 was to become Jackie Stewart's first championship year. The Scot had served a hard, frustrating Formula 1 apprenticeship in the works BRM team, his first season of comparative success in 1965 quickly followed by two wretched years wrestling with cumbersome machinery which wasn't adequate for his talent to shine through. At the end of 1967, he threw off the BRM shackles and joined his long time mentor and guide, Ken Tyrrell, to drive a Matra-Ford in 1968.

Stewart's brilliance was undisputed, but the World Championship was plucked from his grasp in the final race at Mexico City by Graham Hill.

It was a popular title for the British driver, and Stewart certainly didn't begrudge Team Lotus their success. After all, they were still reeling under the effects of the crushing loss of Jimmy Clark at Hockenheim, a tragedy which many people predicted would end Colin Chapman's racing career. But Graham Hill provided Team Lotus with a tower of strength during the troubled months which followed, and everyone agreed that their success was thoroughly deserved.

RONNIE PETERSON

In 1969, Monaco was the third round of the World Championship. Stewart in the Matra MS80 had walked away with the South African Grand Prix at Kyalami, inherited a lucky win in the Spanish Grand Prix and arrived in the Mediterranean principality nursing a comfortable points lead over reigning title holder Hill. Even though he wasn't destined to win at Monaco, this would be the season in which the canny Scot's ability matched with Tyrrell's shrewd judgement took them to their first World Championship together. As he walked from the Hotel de Paris, arm in arm with his wife Helen, it's doubtful whether he even remembered that his first international victory outside England was scored over the same streets some five years earlier.

In 1964 he was a fledgling star in the international arena, driving for Tyrrell in a little BMC engined Formula Three Cooper. The day after this victory endorsed the young Scot's fast rising ability, he watched Graham Hill win the Monaco Grand Prix for BRM. Now he faced Hill's Lotus alongside his Matra on the front row of the grid. Time had passed. He, Jochen Rindt and Jacky Ickx were the acknowledged new stars of motor racing's most exalted stamping ground. The future would look after itself.

If the Monaco Grand Prix was a yardstick of world class driving ability, then the Formula 3 race which always takes place on the Saturday is inevitably a melting pot of aspiring talent. In 1968 it had been won by Henri Pescarolo, the previous year by Jean-Pierre Beltoise, the dour Frenchman who now partnered Stewart in the Tyrrell Matra team. Now there was another bunch of bright eyed newcomers assembling to do battle, all intent on taking another steady step on the path to the top. Inevitably their progress would be closely scrutinised.

Amongst the informed spectators at Monaco was Alan Rees, a perceptive, unobtrusive little man who has been recognised as one of the great racing talent-spotters of the last ten years. Racing was Rees' trade and had been so for more than ten years. In the early and middle 1960s, he had been one of England's most promising single seater competitors, but now he had tired of driving. He realised that his aspirations were not going to be fulfilled. A drive at the wheel of the spare works Cooper-Maserati, arranged by his friend Jochen Rindt, in the British Grand Prix of 1967, left him with the conviction that he wasn't destined to earn a regular Formula One drive. Almost reluctantly he soldiered on in Formula Two, driving the second Winkelmann Racing Brabham alongside Rindt. Finally, he stopped racing at the end of 1968.

Rees' greatest claim to distinction had been achieved outside the cockpit of a racing car. He was the man who first recognised Rindt's true talent and was quick to channel it into Roy Winkelmann's Formula 2 team. Thus, while Rindt grappled with four barren Grand Prix seasons at the wheel of indifferent cars, Rees masterminded the operation which enabled Jochen to win 19 Formula Two events prior to the start of 1969. Their last victory had been at Thruxton on Easter Monday with the new Lotus 59. Now Rees was on another talent-spotting errand. But not for Winkelmann Racing.

Although still closely tied to the Rindt Formula Two team, Rees was involved in the formation of a brand new racing organisation. Though he wasn't to know it, - and if he had, he probably wouldn't have believed it - there would be five Grand Prix cars built by this new concern on the grid at Monte Carlo just twelve months later. But for the moment Rees was looking for a driver to grow within the framework of that new concern, and several Formula 3 drivers were to come under his scrutiny. The organisation was eventually titled March Engineering.

"We wanted a Stewart or a Rindt" Rees later emphasised. "But how in heaven's name were we going to get one. There didn't seem any way at the time, even though we had complicated arrangements going with Rindt". In fact, Robin Herd, who subsequently became March's designer and one of the directors, had been approached directly by Rindt to build him a Formula 1 car under very generous financial terms. But Max Mosley, eloquent barrister partner in the proposed arrangement, could see a great financial basis for the company in the construction of production cars. He pushed for a broad development along several fronts and, from this prospect, Rindt shyed away. "Absolutely typical Jochen" recalls Rees "If he couldn't control the whole deal, then he just didn't want to know".

Against this backcloth of behind-the-scenes strife, Rees was already sifting through the Formula 3 talent and taking careful looks at five drivers in turn. Which one would March choose? Tim Schenken - one of the proto-type 'nice guys' in motor racing who drove the works Formula Three Brabham. Or Howden Ganley, the introspective New Zealander who'd once laid paving stones for Kensington Council as he struggled to raise the cash to buy a racing car. Or Emerson Fittipaldi, the brilliant newcomer from Brazil who was still in Formula Ford. Or Reine Wisell, the Swedish driver of the works Chevron. Or Ronnie Peterson.

For Ronnie Peterson, Monaco's Formula Three race was to provide the most thorough test of his ability so far. Next year he might be sleeping in a comfortable hotel bed, but for now he had to make do with the cramped quarters in the back of his Mercedes-Benz transporter in which he and his mechanic had travelled up from Rome and the previous weekend's race at Vallelunga. In Southern Italy, his Tecno had faced an insignificant challenge from the locals. He'd won easily. Now he was to face his greatest rivals in the gay surroundings of Monte Carlo in May.

While there was much speculation surrounding just who was the best in Formula 3, there was even more intense argument over which of the two blond Swedes was the best. Wisell or Peterson? It was hard to know, for they'd done a pretty good job of avoiding each other for most of 1969 up until Monaco. Reine took part in what generally could be considered the more important events, Ronnie the rather more 'provincial' races. But, as

Rushing up from Saint Devote at Monte Carlo, 1969, Ronnie's Vick Tecno had just passed Reine Wisell's works Chevron. Peterson won this classic 1-litre Formula 3 tussle with his countryman, attracting the attention of Alan Rees in the process

Sveneric Eriksson interviews Ronnie before the 1974 Swedish GP at Anderstorp.

RONNIE PETERSON

Alan Rees was quick to point out, they were both winning their races by substantial margins. "So, when they both arrived at Monaco, I just had to be there".

The Scandinavian newspapers thrived on the rivalry between the two drivers. Reine, ever since the day he'd put Ronnie through the test session for his competition licence at Karlskoga, felt he was the senior Swede. Inwardly, Ronnie knew otherwise. Few people who were in Monaco will forget that Formula 3 race in 1969. They both won their heats, and from the word go in the final it was Ronnie versus Reine. They touched wheels, bounced off kerbs and locked up brakes in one of the most frantic tussles ever seen round those sunlit streets. Eventually Reine's Chevron went up the escape road at the chicane with just a handful of laps left to go. Ronnie Peterson joined the distinguished list of rising stars to have won Monaco's Formula 3 race. "I knew the bloke had talent" observed Rees after it was all over.

Rees had made up his mind. He would approach Peterson the following weekend when the Swede came over to Crystal Palace for the Spring Bank Holiday Monday International. In the garden party atmosphere which the convivial little London track always seemed to generate, the issue for victory in the Formula Three race turned out to be between Peterson and Tim Schenken. Lap after lap they'd change places along the Bottom Straight of this sinuous little circuit, lined with old wooden sleepers close to its edges and thus scarcely less demanding or potentially damaging than Monaco. Ronnie reckoned that, if he was second coming up to the last corner, he could dive out of Schenken's slipstream on the run up to the finishing line, situated several hundred yards up the following straight. But, as they approached that final turn, the pair came up to lap Ganley's Chevron. Schenken slipped past before the corner, just in front of his Antipodean colleague. Ronnie had to wait and be satisfied with second place.

As Ronnie thoughtfully tugged off his helmet and stood to reflect on the changing fortunes of racing, a man approached him in the gravel-strewn paddock. It was Alan Rees. Conversation was awkward in the extreme, for Ronnie's grasp of the English language was elementary and Rees knew no Swedish. Alan wanted the young Swede to drive in one of the remaining 1969 Formula 2 races in a Winkelmann Lotus 59. But he found himself second in the queue. Painstakingly, Ronnie explained that he was already committed to drive in a Formula Two race for the works Tecno team. But he didn't know whether this was to lead on towards greater things or whether it was just a 'one-off'. Tactfully, he said he would contact Rees after he'd run that race.

The race Tecno invited Ronnie to drive in was the Monza Lottery, a spine-tingling slipstreaming 'blind' round the famous Italian circuit near Milan. Bravery and skill were two essential ingredients for success in this race, and many seasoned Formula Two competitors blanched at the sight of the plucky young Swede dicing it out furiously for the lead. Many shook

Formula 2 debut for Peterson in a works Tecno at the 1969 Monza Lottery Grand Prix. He led the race but eventually finished seventh after a pit stop

their heads in doubt, predicting that Peterson would have a big accident if he continued to drive like that. Others, who were wiser and could recognise true talent, stayed silent.

From a grid position mid-way down the field, Ronnie battled his way to the front and actually led the race for several laps. On one lap he let his Tecno slide just too wide as he hurtled through the 140 mph Lesmo curve and a shower of sparks flew from his left front wheel as it clanged against the barrier. "It was only a touch" Ronnie insisted afterwards, "I just kissed it". But the impact was sufficient to bend a steering arm slightly and Ronnie, thinking he had a puncture, stopped in the pits for the car to be checked. He resumed to finish seventh, although at the time of his slight error he'd been running ahead of eventual victor Robin Widdows.

Side by side round the sleeper-lined Crystal Palace circuit go Ronnie (No. 6) and Tim Schenken's works Brabham BT28. Tim beat Ronnie to the flag by a length after Ganley's Chevron got in their way on the last corner

Meanwhile the future directors of March Engineering, as the new company would eventually be known, were still juggling around their possible commitments for 1970. Jochen Rindt was fed up with Lotus and doing his level best to drive a wedge between Rees, Mosley and Herd by continually tantalising the last-named with a Grand Prix project of his own, without the other two participating. Mosley's diplomatic talents were being stretched to bursting point in his efforts to counter Rindt's advances and keep the triumvirate intact. Finally Herd swung decisively round against a proposed liason with Rindt, finally committing himself to work with Rees, Mosley and Graham Coaker, himself an amateur Formula 3 driver. Even though Rees was still ostensibly managing the Winkelmann team in Formula Two, Rindt now realised that his erstwhile team mate's future lay elsewhere.

Back in his own Formula 3 Tecno at Karlskoga in 1969 ....

March resigned themselves to a future without Rindt, Rindt resigned himself staying with Lotus. As for Robin Herd, he always remained slightly reflective that he never took up the chance with Jochen. "For certain obvious reasons I'd have liked to do it" he sighed nearly five years afterwards "because I'd have been just a designer, not obliged to run a business as well. I'd like to think that some of March's designs had suffered because of this". As he spoke he looked upwards to a colour painting of Stewart and Amon leading Monaco in 1970. They were both in March 701s. "Not bad for cars that only cost £2500 a time to build". He grinned his sheepish smile. That picture was always a great favourite of Robin's, probably because it embodied everything that he'd hoped for as a racing car designer and not quite fully achieved.

The progress, success and disappointment which the March quartet would face in the years to follow, could hardly have been envisaged in that enthusiasm with which they started in 1969. Rees renewed his pursuit of **39**

... leading Tetsu Ikuzawa's Lotus 59, Peter Gaydon's Tecno and Howden Ganley's Chevron

A taste of power–driving Jo Bonnier's 5.7-litre Lola-Chevrolet T70 GT at Karlskoga in 1969

Peterson. With a common purpose in mind, he collaborated with Mosley in an effort to get Peterson into Max's Formula Two Lotus for the race at Albi in September. Max, by now certain that he was a better barrister than a professional driver, didn't need much persuading. His Lotus had dumped him in the scenery at Nurburgring back in May and he'd never seemed very keen from that day onward. Ronnie agreed, so three Lotus 59s made the trip down to Albi, near Toulouse, for the race in early September.

Situated in a very pleasant area of France, nobody could call the Albi circuit the most exciting they've ever seen. Originally a road circuit run over closed public highways, the permanent track was opened in the late 1950s and has hosted Formula Two and Three events ever since. It has three long, fast straights joined by fast, bumpy corners. For the wealthy, it's very convenient, as a small airstrip is contained within the circuit's perimeter. Small aircraft doing circuits and bumps vie with the racing cars for attention. Albi has a predominantly friendly atmosphere.

Three Lotus 59s duly appeared at Albi, for Rindt, Hill and Peterson. Ronnie finished fifth in this, his second Formula Two race after a troubled ride. But Rees had seen enough in practice to convince himself that Ronnie was a World Champion in the making. So had Brian Hart, one of England's leading race engine builders and himself a capable Formula Two driver. He was an old friend of Alan's and, hearing that Ronnie was to drive at Albi, had jumped into his Ford Escort and blasted the tedious nine hours down to South West France to watch.

What made up their minds was Ronnie's performance in practice. "I just couldn't believe it" says Rees. "Ronnie happened to go out of the pits during a rain shower in practice and came up onto the tail of Stewart's Matra, and Ronnie kept up with him for five laps on a soaking track. You could see Stewart glancing in his mirrors to try and work out who was chasing him. He could see it was one of our Lotuses, but it wasn't Hill or Rindt driving it. That's a real test of a driver, the wet, and Stewart had to come into the pits to finally get rid of him. I was one hundred per cent sure that Ronnie would win Grand Prix races on the strength of those five laps. It wasn't just speculation; it was obvious!"

On the face of it, there was a surplus of Grand Prix talent at the end of 1969. Lotus were homing in on the obvious abilities of Emerson Fittipaldi, now firmly established as a leading light in Formula Three after just half a season. The highly professional Brabham equipe were clearly grooming Schenken, while both Ganley and Wisell were being tutored by the diligent Bruce McLaren. Many people seemed surprised that Ronnie's future plans were not the subject of more offers from other teams. He openly acknowledges that only March showed a persistent interest in his services for 1970. So, after that race at Albi, Ronnie Peterson committed himself to a contract which, in three years, was destined to take his name, and that of March Engineering, into the limelight of Grand Prix racing.

The first time Alan Rees realised that he was tutoring a future Grand Prix winner was at Albi in late 1969 where Ronnie drove Max Mosley's Lotus 59 entered by Winkelmann Racing to 5th place. Here he leads the late Francois Cevert in a works Tecno

The very first March made its debut in the September International at Cadwell Park. It was a stubby little Formula Three car which used Lotus wheel rims, very conventional in appearance and configuration. Ronnie was at the wheel, and the uninformed enthusiast would have been excused for thinking it was a neat special built by a private owner. But when the March plans became public in the motor sporting press the following week, even Mosley, Herd, Rees and Coaker shuddered slightly. They pledged themselves to build Formula 1 cars for Amon, Siffert and Peterson, plus a works Formula Two and Formula Three team. They'd also build a full range of customer cars in most categories as well.

March Engineering, like Topsy, just grew and grew. Ronnie was the one around whom the directors could see their long-term future revolving, but Mosley's business acumen told him that an established star must be recruited to lead the works team. Thus, with all prospects of Jochen Rindt having disappeared, he started to talk with Chris Amon.

First time out in the prototype March 693 at the Cadwell Park Formula 3 international at the end of 1969. Ronnie (No. 2) just beats Jean-Pierre Jaussaud (Tecno No. 7) and Tim Schenken (Brabham No. 1). On the second row can be seen Mike Beuttler (Brabham No. 16) and the nose of Cyd Williams' Chevron (No. 19). Peterson might have won the race - as it was a punctured tyre helped relegate him to 3rd

Amon was in a similar plight to Rindt. He was only 26 years old, the same age as Ronnie, but he'd been a regular Grand Prix driver for Ferrari since the start of 1967. And it just seemed as though the Gods had ordained that he was never to win a Grand Prix. Tired out with hollow promises from Ferrari, Amon was fascinated by the prospect of a Cosworth engined Grand Prix car. His talks with Mosley grew serious.

It almost seemed as though Peterson had been forgotten as the March directors plunged headlong into Formula One. Ken Tyrrell, left with the choice of staying with Matra and using their V12 in preference to the Cosworth V8 or quitting the Matra fold altogether, took the latter step and Jackie Stewart with him. A few weeks of high pressure talking by Mosley backed up with determined resolution from Rees that Tyrrell had no choice but to buy the March, meant that there would now be four March 701s on the circuit next year. Then Porsche came along with a big 'bag of gold' to instal Jo Siffert in the second works car in a final effort to prevent him leaving their prototype team for Ferrari. March, quick as ever to appreciate the commercial possibilities, grasped Siffert's Porsche money with both hands. STP came into the deal as the works team's backers, and they took a car to run on their own for Mario Andretti. It looked as though Ronnie Peterson would be slid back into the shadows.

Meanwhile, Ronnie had been going about his business with the proto-type Formula Three car. The debut at Cadwell Park was encouraging, ending with a third place and, but for a puncture, would probably have won. But the following week, on the 693s first overseas' outing, Ronnie was fortunate to escape with superficial injuries from what amounted to the most serious accident of his career up to that time.

The race in question took place at the Parisian circuit of Montlhery, a track which had seen better days and by the end of 1969 hosted only a couple of international events each year. The most absurd aspect of its configuration was the inclusion of a straw bale chicane, and this was almost Ronnie's undoing. Racing hard in the leading bunch, Ronnie clipped one of the bales with a wheel of his March, instantly upturning the car. As it rolled over onto its back, a broken suspension wishbone pierced the end of the car's fuel tank. It skated down the circuit upside down, Ronnie pinned beneath it. Inevitably, sparks caused the wreckage to catch fire and it was only through the bravery of some marshals and Ronnie's mechanic Ray Wardell, who ran to the accident from the nearby pits, that he escaped with minor burns to his wrists and arms. Rees, Herd and Mosley were in the signalling pits on the opposite side of the circuit and never witnessed the crash. "Jesus, he was lucky" sighed Rees as he surveyed the wrecked car, "His story should have ended there and then".

Ronnie returned home to his native Orebro to convalesce after a couple of days in hospital. He had a lot on his mind, seriously wondering whether he had made the right decision or not to sign for March. Certainly their prototype Formula Three car was good, but even Ronnie realised that building a Grand Prix car was a very different matter indeed. The realisation that Robin Herd must have felt much the same could have provided little solace for Ronnie, wintering in Sweden. It wasn't that he doubted their word. It was just that so many people around him in racing, were publicly airing their opinion that March couldn't possibly fulfil their announced obligations. All he could do was to wait and to wonder.

The fact that critics were giving March a hard time in the press merely strengthened Mosley's resolution that the cars would appear as and when he announced. Throughout the winter Herd frantically designed and the staff at March's spacious new factory in Bicester toiled away relentlessly. Ronnie was cabled to be at Silverstone on Friday February 5th, where a single works car and a single Tyrrell car would be ready for the world to see. Mosley was as good as his word, and two cars appeared at the bleak Northamptonshire airfield to which winter had chosen to donate an untypical sunny sky, as if to herald in a successful new firm to Grand Prix racing. As one cynic remarked at the time, it seemed as though nature was on the side of these upstarts as well.

The television cameras whirred away at Silverstone that afternoon. And they weren't just from the British television networks, interest in Ronnie's progress was running at a high level in his native Sweden and television interviewers joined him for a brief chat after his first tentative laps at the wheel of Siffert's 701. Ronnie publicly expressed himself satisfied, although privately he remarked "Christ, there's no way I'm ever going to be able to drive this thing. It's so bloody fast".

Little did he know, but Jackie Stewart was already thinking much the same, although not due to the March's speed. Even before the season was under way, the reigning World Champion was feeling reservations about the car which circumstances had thrust upon him. For Ronnie, there were no preconceptions as to how a Grand Prix car should handle. His only opinion was that the damned thing was "so bloody fast".

Just over a month after the March 701s were shown off to the press at Silverstone, Jackie Stewart and Chris Amon started the South African Grand Prix at Kyalami from equal pole position. Max Mosley and Robin Herd preened themselves, outwardly beaming with confidence and reminding the doubters that this was only what they'd expected. Inwardly they were cautious, not having banked on this sort of success. Some clouds of doubt flickered across their sky when Stewart could only muster third place behind Brabham's Brabham BT33 and Hulme's McLaren M14. Still, it was good enough for a start.

Ronnie contented himself with a trip to Malmo and the 'Motor 70' Show organised by his friend and business manager Sveneric Eriksson. Jackie Stewart flew up from Kyalami, where he'd stayed-on after the Grand Prix to take in some tyre testing, to present Ronnie with the 'Motor Man of the

Year' award from a panel of Swedish journalists. Reine Wisell had been the recipient the previous year and was amongst the guests to watch Ronnie receive the acclaim. So were Jo Bonnier, rally ace Bjorn Waldegaard, Tim Schenken and Howden Ganley. Amongst the exhibits was a Formula Three March, ironically enough. Ronnie Peterson, Sweden's most promising racing driver, looked as though he would be without a car. News that McLaren Racing had decided to give Reine Wisell his Formula One baptism at Silverstone in the International Trophy on April 12th didn't exactly encourage Ronnie either.

But Max, Robin and Alan were as good as their word. They'd agreed that Ronnie was to be 'their man' and, somehow or other, they'd find him a car. But things didn't look too hopeful from the outside when there was no Formula Two car for Ronnie at Thruxton on Easter Monday either. It didn't seem to bother Ronnie too much after he'd tried the bulbous 702 in Saturday practice, though. "You only had to look at the 702 to see that it was two years behind in design" remarked Ronnie in one of his more philosophical moods. Robin Herd didn't need much telling, he could work things out for himself. Rindt put the new Lotus 69 onto pole position in 1 m 14.8s. Ronnie's best in the unofficial session was 1 m 19s. Everyone knew Ronnie was better than that. "Promising, but unsorted" wrote *Motoring News* at the time. "I think that's putting it too politely" grinned Herd nervously.

Everyone waited impatiently for Ronnie's 701 to materialise, and the March directors' confidence in their car was shaken on 6th when Colin Chapman unveiled his new Lotus 72. This was the car which would put Jochen Rindt on the pinnacle of Formula One achievement as the fastest Grand Prix driver. Three years later it would do the same for Ronnie Peterson.

But envy over Rindt's new machine didn't even flash across Ronnie's mind. He was just so anxious to see his own Formula One car. "Max, Robin and Alan stuck to the deal they'd done with me. They really were good to me. They promised that I'd have a car, and even after Siffert arrived, they stood by their word. I'm certain that if I'd been anywhere else, they'd have pushed me out". Ronnie's clinging faith in March was rewarded at the start of April, 1970, when it was announced that Colin Crabbe, a distinguished English historic car fanatic, would run Peterson's 701 under the banner of Antique Automobiles, the firm which he runs dealing in ancient and exotic road cars.

Crabbe had entered a Cooper-Maserati V12 and subsequently a McLaren for Vic Elford during the 1969 Grand Prix season, but this liason had been brought to a premature finish at the German Grand Prix where Elford crashed into the remains of Andretti's four-wheel drive Lotus on the opening lap and broke his shoulder seriously. Now, with works backing, Crabbe was facing his second Grand Prix season with a car that was an unknown quantity and a newcomer to Formula One.

Some days things just don't go right. Ronnie cannons over the banking at Mallory Park at
the start of 1971, his works March having seized a steering arm ball joint while he was leading the opening international of the British calendar

"It was good to be with Crabbe" recalls Ronnie, "we had just one car
and one engine. Nobody was expecting me to win, so I had a year in which
to learn. We'd only got the one engine, and it wasn't always rebuilt between
races, so it wasn't that perfect". Nevertheless, Ronnie Peterson, Grand Prix
driver, had a Formula One car at last. And it was to Monaco he hastened for
his Grand Prix debut accompanied by his delightful, blonde girlfriend
Barbro. This time he had the luxury of a hotel room!

Of all the races that Ronnie would run in the Formula One car
during 1970, the Monaco Grand Prix proved to be the best. March's newcomer found that a Grand Prix car was much heavier, less agile than the
Formula Three Tecno, and he was pushed hard to qualify - "Really, I
shouldn't have had to screw myself up like that!" was Ronnie's slightly
incredulous reaction to the pace of Formula One.

Nevertheless, his practice time looked respectable. He lapped in 1 m 26.8s to qualify in his very first Grand Prix while Stewart, albeit on different tyres, earned pole position in his Tyrrell March in 1 m 24s dead. Neither Stewart nor Amon finished, Brabham handed Rindt the victory laurels on the last corner when he slid into the barrier and Ronnie Peterson finished seventh. "Monaco always seems to be quite a good place for me".

Monaco certainly had been a good place in 1970 as well. Ronnie's Grand Prix debut was closely scrutinised by Ferrari's team manager Dr Franco Gozzi and the sandy haired Swede immediately clicked in his mind as a possibility for the Maranello sports car team. Chris Amon, probably relieved that Ferrari machinations no longer affected his fortunes, put in a good word for Ronnie. An invitation was duly made for him to come to Modena and try a 512.

Modena's old race track hasn't been used for racing since 1960. In the centre of this drab North Italian town, it's encased within high walls and doubles as the local flying school, a business which maintains some of the most precarious old planes imaginable. The track gates are perpetually open, so anybody who tests there will have an attendant escort of scruffy little children tagging along behind. Occasionally Ferrari shuts the gates, and the urchins have to perch along the top of a crumbling brick wall to catch a glimpse of his blood red cars. Modena has an atmosphere of decay about it.

Peterson arrived at Modena to try the 5-litre Ferrari 512, a car which was frantically vying with Porsche's flat-12 cylinder 917 for honours in the long distance sports car races. Several drivers who have experience of both cars feel that the Ferrari was virtually as good a car as its rival, but superior organisation of the teams operating the German cars made them more consistently effective. So it was to prove at Le Mans, the sole race in which Ronnie drove a 512.

Ronnie's first impression was that the Ferrari was "big, fast and heavy". Obviously it was appreciably less responsive than his nimble Grand Prix March, but he was impressed by its track manners, likening it to the Bonnier Lola which he'd driven at Karlskoga the previous year. But there certainly wasn't enough room in the cockpit and Ronnie found himself sitting with his head cocked to the left in order that the mechanics could close the door. It was fine on left handers, but useless on right handers. Ronnie agreed to drive, making a mental note as to how important a co-driver of similar height would be in a long distance race. Just over a year later, when signing for Ferrari's 3-litre prototype team, he recalled this incident and that's one of three reasons why his co-driver in 1972 was his old Formula Three colleague Tim Schenken. "He's a good driver, a good friend ... and the same height" was Ronnie's advice to Ferrari.

For the Ferrari team, Le Mans was a catastrophe. Clay Regazzoni, Mike Parkes and Reine Wisell managed to collide with each other after just over three hours racing. Derek Bell, sharing the 512 with Peterson, dropped

49

his clutch and blew up the engine trying to avoid the chaos. "He probably pressed the clutch in fright" Ronnie grimaced. But at least he was at Le Mans. A week earlier, after an unpleasant incident with a traffic policeman at the Belgian Grand Prix it looked as though Ronnie might be in prison instead.

Grand Prix racing was going through a politically turbulent time in 1970. Racing at the super-fast Spa Francorchamps circuit had become one of the major hobby horses of the Grand Prix Drivers Association, and there was some valid doubt as to whether they would agree to race if it was raining. Four years earlier, over half the field had been eliminated in a first lap accident when a belt of rain doused half the circuit shortly before the start. Jackie Stewart had suffered the most serious injuries of his career, fortunately only a broken shoulder and some fuel burns, and he was dead-set against the whole affair. Minor circuit alterations to reduce the speed at which cars went onto the 180 mph-plus Masta straight only paid superficial lip service to the question of safety. Either you accepted Spa as it was, like Pedro Rodriguez, who did, and won. Or you grinned and bore it, like most of the others. Ronnie personally liked Spa a lot and wanted to practice as much as he could, but the main issue surrounding circuit safety was the province of established stars. Peterson wanted to motor race.

Leaving a nearby hotel at the wheel of his Mercedes Ronnie swung along the outside of a long traffic queue which appeared to be stretching way past the turning down to the track. He nipped down the outside for 100 yards and then tried to swing left to enter the circuit approach. But the policeman on point duty wasn't having it. So, when he looked the other way, Ronnie just went!

"I was chased by a motorcycle policeman and brought back up to the point duty fellow. He really was getting very excited and took me off to the police station where he told them that I'd run over his foot. Even though there was a witness, who said I didn't, they wouldn't believe me". The organisers just managed to realise that they were one car short in time to effect Ronnie's release from the police station and get him into the race. But the policemen were waiting for him at the finish and whisked him back to the police station, still in his grubby old overalls.

Things looked grim after he was consigned to a prison cell for two nights, although he was eventually released on the understanding that he would return for a proper court case later in the summer. It was all a question of lane discipline and the whole affair was finally resolved with the case being dismissed, Ronnie shaking hands with his policeman friend and the Belgian Government paying all his legal expenses. The matter was forgotten.

Ronnie's first year in Formula One provided him with the grounding he needed to make a real impact on the Grand Prix scene the following year, even though most of his 1970 drivers were unobtrusive and others found

CHAPTER 1

Chapman, to become a prime mover in Ronnie's career, shares a joke

their way into the limelight before him. In the French Grand Prix at Clermont Ferrand, he qualified alongside the BRM of Pedro Rodriguez on the fifth row of the grid and ran in the middle of the field until his car's transmission packed up. Next stop was Brands Hatch and the British Grand Prix, a race in which a pit stop dropped him to ninth, just one place behind Lotus debutant Emerson Fittipaldi in his Lotus 49.

51

At the German Grand Prix he retired with engine failure, was forced to miss Austria owing to the engine shortage, retired at both Monza and in Canada. Finally he rounded his first season off with 11th at Watkins Glen, six laps down on winner Fittipaldi who received the victory laurels in just his fourth Grand Prix. On the face of it Peterson had achieved little. But Colin Chapman was impressed enough to talk to him very seriously, even though he'd already contracted Fittipaldi and Wisell for the following year. But they were only exploratory talks. Chapman was in no position to find enough finance to run a third car, and Ronnie's March contract was for three years with an option, on the part of the March directors, at the end of the first two years.

Mosley, Herd and Rees were under no illusion that they wanted Ronnie for 1971. Somehow the 701 saga, which looked so promising both at Kyalami and Monaco, had turned against them. Stewart's misgivings about the machine ended with Tyrrell building his own car, the advent of Rindt in a competitive Lotus 72 had continued to stack the odds against them and the last straw was Chris Amon's disappointment in the team. Amon had complained about the car for much of the year, argued with Herd and Mosley in no uncertain terms. He spoke seriously to Matra and then took the decision to leave and join the French team. He had no conviction left about the March.

It was interesting to notice how the experienced drivers, those who had sampled other Formula 1 machines, criticised the March's handling. Stewart complained that it was impossible to drive smoothly, Amon thought it was hopeless and both Siffert and Andretti were bewildered. Neither Ronnie nor Francois Cevert, Tyrrell's number two who replaced Johnny Servoz when he retired after Monaco, had any yardstick with which to judge the March. They seemed distinctly less inhibited by the car.

Stewart had the last word on the 701. He played golf with Robin Herd shortly before practice at the Canadian Grand Prix. Robin suggested that if Jackie won the game, then he would drive the Tyrrell, if he did not then he should drive the March. With three holes left to play, Herd was one up and, with practice starting shortly, suggested that they call it a day there and then. Stewart said to him with a horrified expression; "Robin. Never has anyone had such an incentive not to lose a golf match before". They played it out. Stewart finished one up and raced the Tyrrell!

The March 701 will be remembered as one of the real 'instant' Grand Prix cars. One person who was absolutely convinced that to drive one would be a passport to Grand Prix fame, was German Formula Two driver Hubert Hahne. He arrived at Bicester, handed over the required amount of Deutschmarks and drove off with the car in the general direction of Hockenheim, venue for the German Grand Prix. He didn't qualify. But Mr Hahne didn't seem to be able to grasp that the inability to qualify was a reflection on him and not the car. He had been swindled, Hahne decided, and the works March transporter found itself shadowed by police helicopters all the way up the autobahn after the race and impounded at the frontier. Clearly, alleged Hahne, he hadn't been sold one of the 'proper' cars.

Max Mosley, suppressing his indignant anger, sorted the whole matter out. But Hahne wanted proof that his car was a competitive machine. The deal was that Ronnie would take it to Silverstone and lap at a prescribed speed, a speed which he'd already managed in his own March. Only the thinnest wedge of doubt filtered across Mosley's mind that day as Ronnie prepared to vindicate his employers. No, Mosley decided he wouldn't worry, it was not possible that Ronnie could fail them. He didn't. He lapped almost two seconds quicker than the prescribed speed. Hahne, looking very thoughtful, returned to Germany and announced his retirement from racing.

By the end of 1970 March was alone. The 'bullshit racers' as they'd been unkindly dubbed had been humbled. Those precocious newcomers who'd lured top names like Amon and Stewart and who'd looked set to shake the Formula 1 world in their first race, had been reduced to the status of also-rans. Honour had been satisfied as far as the establishment was concerned.

Max Mosley didn't like the stigma some people were trying to attach to March's first-season efforts. Inwardly he couldn't make his mind up whether they were established or not. Robin Herd was working hard on a brand new design for 1971, the semi-streamlined 711, and Ronnie Peterson was told, shortly after the Mexican Grand Prix, that he would be the works number one driver in his second season of Formula One racing.

Once more, Mosley set out on a 'deal raising' trip and his first port of call was Alfa Romeo. Before very long March announced that a number one, Cosworth engined 711 would be driven by Ronnie Peterson and a second car, fitted with the Alfa Romeo V8 engine tried by McLaren Racing the previous year, would be shared between Andrea de Adamich and Nanni Galli. The deal was for free engines from Alfa, an arrangement which Mosley hoped might lead to the development of their flat-12 motor for March's Formula 1 cars the following year. But as the Alfa engined McLaren had only once actually managed to qualify for a Grand Prix, and on that one occasion it failed to start anyway, developments along these lines didn't seem very promising at all.

March went to South Africa to carry out a lot of testing prior to the South African Grand Prix and, although he failed to finish the race, Ronnie felt confident of the season ahead. He had found his feet at the wheel of a Grand Prix car and, still rather quietly, developed a growing self-assurance. He still felt the protective veneer generated by the three March directors: Herd, Mosley and Rees also felt more confident. The 711 looked very good; now they would take on the world with 'their' driver.

Ronnie's resilience was put to the test shortly after he went to South Africa. He drove the March 711 in its British debut at the Race of Champions at Brands Hatch the week prior to the South African race. It wasn't a works car, but a private entry which had been sold to Frank Williams for Henri Pescarolo to drive, and it was fitted with inboard front brakes in line with Herd's original design. The car wasn't finished in time for official practice, but Ronnie started from the back of the grid. He was catching up well when one of the shafts operating the inboard brakes snapped under braking for Clearways. "The bloody thing just turned right" Peterson snapped to inquisitive glances. Herd changed all the remaining 711s to outboard front brakes immediately and they never reverted!

Herd's new Formula Two car, the 712, was shaping well. After the cumbersome and bulky 702, the 1971 chassis was designed to provide Ronnie with the tool to win the European Championship as well as a popular buy for private owners. First time out, at Mallory Park, Ronnie's 712 turned sharp left as he swept into the almost flat-out Esses when a ball joint on the end of a steering arm seized. The car ended upside down on the bank with Ronnie trapped underneath it; he emerged, looking very angry, with just a cut on the back of one of his hands. He'd been leading the race comfortably at the time.

Motor racing is a fickle business. If anyone has more than a couple of crashes within a few weeks of each other, then they're dubbed a 'crasher' or 'car breaker'. Ronnie found all sorts of allegations being made against him in the press at this time, saying he had no mechanical sympathy or that he wasn't sufficiently restrained. He felt frustrated and his shortage of results aggravated the situation. He wanted to win and he knew very well that he could. But there was even more disappointment waiting for him at Silverstone in May.

The week after retiring from the Nurburgring Formula 2 race, Ronnie was entered at the non-championship International Trophy meeting at Silverstone, a combined race of Formula One and Formula 5000 cars. For that one race he was given a try in the March-Alfa Romeo which had originally been entered for Nanni Galli. The Italian V8 was performing surprisingly well and Ronnie found that it would rev to 10,000 rpm quite easily on sections where his Cosworth only managed 9,600 rpm. "Take it to 10,600" grinned Mosley. "I can't" replied Ronnie" It starts to make a funny noise at around 10,400!" Funny noise or not, Ronnie managed to qualify the March-Alfa in the middle of the second row for the first 26 lap heat.

The car didn't live up to expectations, and a quick pit stop to secure an electrical lead dropped Ronnie right to the back of the field. A few laps from the end of the heat Ronnie went missing. Approaching Becketts, a fast third gear right hander, something broke in the throttle mechanism of the Alfa Romeo engine and jammed it wide open. Ronnie didn't have a chance to take the corner. The March ran wide onto the grass and slammed into the bank.

One of the front wheels whiplashed back and caught Ronnie a glan-

Another lucky escape at Silverstone in the STP March-Alfa V8. Amidst a shower of mud and stones, Ronnie slams into the bank after a throttle linkage failure

cing blow on the side of his crash helmet. He lay unconscious in the car for several moments until a photographer arrived and tried to release him. Then marshals came on the scene, and an ambulance. He was bundled into the back and, with Debbie Rees to keep him company, driven to Northampton hospital. He was kept overnight for observation. Ronnie regained consciousness in the ambulance and Debbie had to tell him what had happened!

March Engineering were extremely concerned, Rees voicing very serious doubts as to whether he should compete in the Formula Two race at Madrid the following weekend. But Ronnie is a tenacious individual, and despite a good deal of pain from his ribcage, flew out to Madrid on the Tuesday after his Silverstone accident. The medical authorities at the Spanish track got to hear of it and insisted he had a full medical examination before they would let him take part. He passed the medical, but his car failed in the race and another non-finisher was recorded in the record book.

55

RONNIE PETERSON

Then it was back to Monaco. Ronnie was just about at an all-time low as far as racing was concerned. Not a person to show much outward sensitivity, he became openly absent in his manner during the early part of the European season. He didn't want to waste time talking with anyone who wasn't directly involved in his racing activities. It wasn't that he was being anti-social, it was simply that he had become so immersed, so involved in trying to break out of this bad luck streak, that he had no time for anything else.

"Monaco seems to be quite a good place for me" reflected Ronnie. In 1968, 69, 70, 71 and 73 it was the race in which I got my first big break of the year". And 1971 was certainly no exception, in fact it was one of the most important Grand Prix races of Peterson's career. It was the one in which he finally scored his first helping of World Championship points.

The March 711 handled extremely well round the streets of the Principality. In practice Ronnie felt he could have improved on his fourth row qualifying time "but Robin was messing about with copper brake discs and I ran out of brakes halfway through the session. By the time we'd changed them there wasn't any time left".

Jackie Stewart devastated the opposition that year at Monaco. Despite a slight brake imbalance, he led from start to finish. The only other competitor who looked remotely in the flying Scot's class was Ronnie Peterson. Driving with terrific maturity, he defeated the highly rated BRMs of Jo Siffert and Pedro Rodriguez, Denny Hulme's McLaren and the flat-12 Ferrari of Jacky Ickx.

Ronnie tells the tale; "It was a huge dice with Pedro Rodriguez and Denny. I managed to slip past Denny, but Pedro's blocking was just incredible. Absolutely incredible. Eventually I had to force him to brake so late into the Gasworks hairpin that his BRM came out with square wheels. He had to limp into the pits to change them; all four!"

By this stage Siffert, Ickx and Stewart were going away in front of the works March. Enthusiastic spectators watched the scarlet car carefully to see whether the young Swede would rise to the occasion or clip a kerb and limp into ignominious retirement. But Ronnie was displaying a new-found maturity. The red March quickly homed in on Siffert and then on Ickx who obligingly let him go past his ailing Ferrari. Then it was just Jackie Stewart who lay between Peterson and his first Grand Prix triumph. But the Scot had consolidated such a lead that there was no way in which Ronnie could get to terms with the French-blue Tyrrell. Even a momentary lapse by the brilliant Stewart, when he ran wide coming out of the Tabac turn and brushed the barrier with his left hand wheels had no more than a momentary influence on his lead.

Ronnie's natural tenacity told him that he should keep trying, but his reasoning made him realise that only mechanical failure could rob Stewart of his second triumph at the picture postcard circuit. His March was shaving tenths of a second off Stewart's advantage on every lap, but eventually Ronnie prudently slowed to make sure of that hard won second place. The March pit received their hero with tumultuous applause. Mosley, Herd and Rees beamed happily. 'Their' driver had done it. The only shadow to be cast over the weekend was the news from England that Graham Coaker had died in hospital in Northampton. Graham had left the company a few months earlier and, in his spare time, returned to his love of club racing. He'd acquired a March 712 as part of his financial settlement with the other directors, but crashed it at the Easter Silverstone meeting and sustained a broken leg. A few days before Ronnie's terrific Monaco performance Graham died from complications which set in as a result of an operation.

Trying to start Frank Williams' March 711 just before the 1971 Race of Champions. Ronnie set off late from the starting grid and was pulling up through the field before the failure of an inboard front brake shaft brought about an alarming moment under braking for Clearways and his retirement from the race

Ronnie drove this Scuderia Filipinetti 2-litre Lola T212 into a splendid second place behind Toine Hezeman's DART Chevron in the 1971 Martini International at Silverstone

A cockpit shot of Ronnie at work in the March-Cosworth 711 during the 1971 Spanish Grand Prix in Barcelona's picturesque Montjuich Park

RONNIE PETERSON

The rest of 1971 simply served to build up the confidence of March's directors as well as setting Peterson on a pinnacle. He wasn't to win a Grand Prix, but justly became recognised as a mature Grand Prix driver. Eventually March's success in 1971 peculiarly caused Peterson to leave them. The 711 enabled Ronnie to take storming second places at Silverstone, Monza and Mosport Park by the end of that season. He also ended runner-up to Stewart in the World Championship. On paper, anything less than the World Championship crown would be a disappointment in 1972.

Third place in the streaming rain at Zandvoort behind those acknowledged wet weather experts Ickx and Rodriguez, added another page to Peterson's 1971 success story, but the French Grand Prix at Paul Ricard placed an ugly blemish on the scoresheet.

Mosley and Rees were increasingly at odds with each other. Rees was more interested in nurturing Ronnie as a potential World Champion, but Mosley's business mind told him that financial stability for March was the most important objective at the time. Mosley, courting Alfa Romeo intently, despite the obvious deficiency displayed by their V8 engine, decreed that Ronnie would run this unit installed in his 711 at Paul Ricard.

Ronnie was absolutely furious, telling Mosley so in no uncertain terms. But Max stuck to his guns. Ronnie was to run with the Alfa unit and that was that. Commercial and economic considerations aside, Ronnie didn't see why he should have his Championship chances jeopardised. He had been going well, and strongly resented Mosley's decision, but it was typical of his willingness and determination that he should hurl the car round Ricard as fast as he could make it go.

The March-Alfa qualified quite respectably on the grid, respectably for the March-Alfa, that is. Every lap Ronnie would be passed by at least one car as he accelerated away from the tight right hander before the pits. Eventually he was running last, a solid and undisputed last. Finally the engine blew up in the biggest possible way, showering the main straight with an oil slick that sent Regazzoni's Ferrari straight off the track. Ronnie walked home. "It was a big bang" he told Alan "but a happy one!"

The record books show that the works March team had yet to win a Grand Prix, just as the record books show that Ronnie Peterson finished second on five occasions in the 1971 World Championship series. But statistics can never tell the full story and the Italian Grand Prix of 1971 will be remembered as the race where Peter Gethin won his sole Grand Prix victory. By less than a tenth of a second from Ronnie Peterson's March.

Monza in September seems to breed drama and excitement. The irrepressible enthusiasm of an excited Italian crowd combined with the magnetic attraction of Grand Prix cars on full song generates a distinctive atmosphere. It doesn't have the class and character of Monaco, nor the intricacy and spectacle of Nurburgring. But Monza is the home of speed. Grand Prix cars are held on full throttle for a matter of half a minute or so at a time.

Nowhere shows up fragility like Monza.

With 51 points to his credit, Jackie Stewart had clinched the World Championship at the Austrian Grand Prix three weeks earlier. But now, with three rounds left to go, a tense dispute for second place was holding the attention of the pundits. Ferrari's team leader Jacky Ickx held second place with 19 points prior to Monza, Peterson had 17 points and Emerson Fittipaldi 16. After an indifferent season, punctuated with just a single Grand Prix triumph, Ferrari's hopes were pinned on Monza for a reversal of fortunes in front of their home crowd. Peterson was fortunate enough to have a brand new Cosworth engine ready for the Italian Grand Prix, even though Robin Herd didn't feel that it would make an appreciable difference to the March. He felt the 711 was already slippery enough to show well along the fast straight of the Italian track.

Despite its long straights, Monza still remains a compromise for modern-day Grand Prix cars. Without the aerodynamic wings to exert down-force on the straight, a great saving in drag is effected. But this shortage of downforce effectively reduces adhesion on corners. A driver and his designer must decide where to draw the line of compromise. Peterson did quite a bit of practice with the front wing on and the front wing off. Eventually they decided that the car would run with no front wing, the bullet-like nose section of the 711 penetrating the air like a knife. The rear wing was wound down into an almost horizontal angle.

Monza, as usual, was packed to capacity on the day of the race. But those thousands of fans who had spent their lira confidently in the hope of a Ferrari victory were bleakly rewarded. Both Ickx and Regazzoni were out before twenty laps had been completed, the flat-12 engines of their Italian cars broken. The crowd hissed with contempt. They had been let down badly, so they looked elsewhere for new heroes to cheer.

Setting a pace as scorching as the September sun overhead, the leading bunch hurtled round the Milanese circuit as if attached by a gigantic thread of elastic. World Champion Stewart was already on his way back to his Lake Como lair, the engine of his Tyrrell having shattered on lap 16. Siffert's BRM fell from the battle with gearbox trouble while his team mate Howden Ganley couldn't make a bid for the lead owing to failing brakes. The new generation of Grand Prix stars were making their name, and it was Ronnie Peterson doing the lion's share of the leading.

In the pits, Mosley and Herd shuddered. They'd been close to victory before, but now Ronnie was about to pull it off. They could hardly bear to watch. The race moved into its final phase. With eight laps to go, Chris Amon, the former March team leader who was still hunting for that elusive first Grand Prix victory, started to flex his muscles. His V12 Matra had started from pole position and Amon fully realised that he could out-run his rivals in the leading bunch. But he would have to wait for the final lap to out-fumble them. Reaching for the grimy, oil-stained top vizor on the front of his helmet, Chris peeled it off and hurled it overboard, intending to leave a clear and clean vizor below. He inadvertently pulled them both off and ruined his chances in the face of a 200 mph breeze.

Amon dropped away. The race was now between Peterson, Tyrrell's number two Francois Cevert and Mike Hallwood in his Surtees TS9. A few lengths further back came Ganley and then there was a long gap to Peter Gethin's BRM. In the intensity of their dice for the lead, none of the leaders noticed Gethin creeping up slowly. Peterson and Cevert both thought they could win. Hailwood thought he probably couldn't, but that wouldn't stop him from having a bloody good try!

"I could pass anyone when I wanted to" explained a sweating Peterson after the race to a silent Mosley. "I was trying to work out how to beat Cevert - he was the one I really had to watch. I knew I must lead into Parabolica because he hadn't the speed to pass me between there and the line". Parabolica is a tricky, almost flat-out right hander which, as its name suggests, swings the cars through 180 degrees and catapults them out onto the home straight. If Cevert led into Parabolica, Ronnie might not beat him to the line.

The crowd, sensing a great occasion, were cheering everybody, anybody who led. With one lap to go, Peterson led Cevert across the start/finish line in a great crash of sound. The man with the chequered flag prepared to do his job. With a broken exhaust pipe, Ronnie was suffering from a slightly down-on-power engine, but he positioned himself beautifully as they braked for Parabolica and sliced inside Cevert's stubby blue Tyrrell for that last sprint to the line.

Just as he swung in, Ronnie checked his mirrors. Suddenly there was a cloud of dust as Gethin's BRM, front tyres chirping, slid and scuffed its way past on the inside. Ronnie's plot had been foiled. The March drifted wide, but stayed more or less alongside the BRM as they rocketed out of the corner. He suddenly realised that the BRM was going to beat him on acceleration, so Ronnie swung the March hard over to the right and glued its nose to Gethin's gearbox. The rev counter needle shot up as the slipstream effect took over. At the end of the pit barrier, not one hundred yards from the chequered flag, Peterson pulled out and tried to surge past as they hurtled towards the line.

But it was fractionally too late. Peter Gethin popped his hand from the cockpit to acknowledge victory as the red March surged alongside. After fifty five hectic, sweating and dusty laps, the end result was just another second place in the result book for Ronnie Peterson. Just another second.

Somehow, although Ronnie subsequently finished in a splendid second place behind Stewart in the wet at Canada, and rounded off his season with a third at Watkins Glen, that race of Monza was the pinnacle of his achievement with the March. It would be unfair to suggest that relations with the March directors deteriorated from that point onwards, but Ronnie

Rolling to a halt after the thrilling 1971 Italian Grand Prix at Monza. Peter Gethin's BRM P160 (in the foreground) has just beaten Ronnie's STP March 711 for victory by one hundredth of a second in one of the most thrilling finishes ever seen at the Italian circuit. Gethin took the lead on the last corner and crossed the line with Peterson's March alongside

never achieved the same sort of storming success again. At the end of 1971, the full realisation dawned on Herd and Mosley that to have a fighting chance of keeping Peterson beyond the end of the following season, they would have to offer him a car capable of winning the World Championship. WIth that objective in mind, Herd began work on the March 721X. Ironically, that became the car which was directly responsible for Ronnie's departure to Lotus.

Part of Mosley's projected deal with Alfa Romeo gave Ronnie the chance of driving one of their sports cars in the 1971 Watkins Glen 6 Hours. He accepted the invitation and duly won the event, co-driving with Andrea de Adamich. Upon his return, Herd quizzed him over the effectiveness of the Alfa Romeo gearbox, a unit mounted between the engine and rear axle line rather than behind the rear axle line. Ronnie acknowledged that it felt "quite good", a reaction Herd was hopefully anticipating, for his plans for the 721X were quite startling. He proposed to use a similarly mounted gearbox on his new Formula One car, the intention being to improve the fundamental stability and controllability of the car by concentrating as much weight as possible within the wheelbase of the car. It was a bold venture which might have worked, had it not been for the adoption of the Alfa gearbox itself.

Modern-day motor racing is such a competitive exercise that few teams have the equipment or facilities to break away from established trends. To maintain a test and development department is a costly business, and Herd's effort with the 721X was quite simply a gamble which failed to come off owing to a shortage of time and resources. Ideally, March should have built their own gearbox unit, but time and pressure dictated that they would be obliged to utilise existing components. Once installed in the car, it became clear that gearchanging was a slow and laborious affair. As Ronnie remarked, the car was quite good. But 'quite good' cars are not good enough to win World Championships.

For 1972, Ronnie Peterson was joined in the March works team by the 23 year old Austrian Niki Lauda. Andy Granatelli's STP Corporation once again extended their sponsorship to back March's works effort for the third year, but Lauda's drive had to be paid for. Having just spent a year in Mosley's Formula Two 'rentaMarch' circus, the ambitious Austrian wanted to drive in Grands Prix. He was called ambitious and precocious at the time. Now he drives for Ferrari as their team leader.

Niki Lauda persuaded an Austrian bank to advance him the necessary £35,000 to 'buy' his way into Grand Prix racing. As a number two to Peterson, Lauda reasoned, he would gain invaluable experience and be in a position to earn a paid drive for 1973. That was his idea, at least. But when he climbed out of the new March 721X at Jarama after two laps' practice for the Spanish Grand Prix, Robin Herd might have been forgiven a degree of consternation on being confronted with the baby-faced Niki saying "No

Struggling gamely with the recalcitrant March 721X in the 1972 Spanish Grand Prix at Jarama, Ronnie trails round in front of Dave Walker's Lotus 72 and Peter Gethin in the equally ungainly BRM P180. The chafed nose section on the STP car is the result of Ronnie spinning in the middle of the field on the opening lap

way, your car is no good".

Peterson was fast arriving at the same conclusion. When he drove the March 721X in its preliminary tests at Silverstone, he felt confident enough. At Brands Hatch the car felt nice to drive in the Race of Champions, but just wasn't recording the times. "It's so slow that I don't believe it" said Ronnie. Robin said it would all be OK, so Ronnie decided to hold his peace.

"It will not work" asserted a disappointed Peterson as he fumbled his way round Jarama. Herd smiled his bland smile. It would be alright soon. Ronnie reflected that soon wasn't going to be soon enough. Emerson Fittipaldi won the Grand Prix from Jacky Ickx in the Ferrari. The March team leader started the race on brand new tyres only to spin in the middle of the second corner. "Why I didn't hit anyone, I just don't bloody know" grimaced Ronnie. "I just want the car fixed".

Herd assured both his drivers that it would be fixed, although inwardly he wasn't quite certain what was wrong. He felt that the problem might be in the differential. That was changed for the Monaco Grand Prix and the car was useless. He felt it could be the gearbox, so that was changed for the Oulton Park Spring Cup. And that didn't make much difference either. Ronnie highlighted that race by being involved in a collision with his old rival Reine Wisell, who was driving a BRM, as they accelerated away from the grid. "As I came up beside him, he pulled over and my rear wheel hit his front wheel" Ronnie insisted. The kick-back through the steering broke one of Wisell's fingers. "That's my story - Reine's got a different one and I'm sure we'll never agree" was Ronnie's verdict.

Ronnie's attention was taken by the adapted Formula Two March which had been built for Mike Beuttler to go Grand Prix racing with. "It's quicker down the straight than my car" he insisted to Robin at the Belgian Grand Prix. By this point, Herd didn't need a lot of convincing that just about anything would be better than the 721X. There had to be some way of salvaging something from this disastrous season, so a test session at Silverstone was arranged immediately after the return from Nivelles. No more proof was needed. With identical gear ratios fitted, Ronnie was more than three seconds a lap quicker in the 721G than he was in the 721X. Mosley and Herd decided that they would build a couple for Peterson and Lauda in time for the French Grand Prix at Clermont Ferrand.

It worked. Ronnie finished fourth at Clermont behind Stewart, Fittipaldi and Amon. The world looked sunny again for March Engineering, but that 'bloody 721X' had done its damage. With less than six months of his March contract left to go, Chapman was watching closely. For the motor racing world, it was almost obvious how the course of events would go over the next few months. Chapman asked Ronnie if he wanted to join Lotus and, despite a feeling of mixed loyalty to March, he could only reply "yes". Chapman felt relieved, Mosley felt apprehensive.

There was no real point in threatening any legal action against anyone offering Ronnie a contract in 1973. But Mosley realised the implications of losing Ronnie. If March were left without him, the way ahead into 1973 would be bleaker than they ever imagined. When Ronnie signed an option in the summer of 1972, to join Lotus if Chapman could raise the necessary money, Mosley lost his cool. He lectured Ronnie about moral obligations, he let it be known that he was consulting lawyers to find a way out of the Swede's commitment. But Ronnie knew what he had done and there wasn't much point in Max consulting any legal advisors on the point. Max was an eminently capable barrister and knew that it was all over the moment he saw Ronnie's option.

Ronnie Peterson signed a two year contract for Team Lotus on August 28th 1972, the same day as Emerson Fittipaldi won the Rothmans 50,000 race for the team at Brands Hatch. Chapman had won, Mosley had lost and, in the weeks which followed, as Ronnie worked out his time driving for March in the three last Grands Prix of the year, Mosley gave him a hard time. He spun all over the place at Monza, he was really upset. But Mosley wasn't really annoyed with Ronnie, he was just annoyed that he had lost the contest with Chapman. Herd had been right, neither of them liked losing.

Two years later, at the Brazilian Grand Prix, March fortunes in Formula One racing were on the rise again. Their new 741 had begun to show great potential in the hands of Hans-Joachim Stuck and both Mosley and Herd smiled freely again. Ronnie trickled past them in his black and gold Lotus. "It's a good car, this 741" grinned Max as if to prime Robin to perform a sort of pre-arranged double-act.

"It'll have to be better" replied Robin, "particularly if we're to get Ronnie back next year". They both laughed. But it would have taken a lot of brusque confidence, even for Mosley, to stroll up to Ronnie and make such a proposal at that time. Even though they both felt he was, in Herd's words, "the best, the quickest and the nicest", Ronnie Peterson's 'three year March' had finished, for good, just over a year earlier.

Through the picturesque streets of the south west France town of Pau, Ronnie's March leads
Francois Cevert's Elf Tecno and Jean-Pierre Beltoise's March during the opening stages of the 1971
race. Both Cevert and Peterson retired early, leaving Beltoise to lead almost to the finish when, he too,
retired. This ironic series of misfortunes handed victory to Reine Wisell in a Lotus 69

CHAPTER 3
King of Formula 2

IN THE LATTER HALF of the 1960s the aim of any Formula 3 driver worth his salt was to make a move into Formula 2. In no way second class as its title might suggest, but a frantic hotchpotch of Grand Prix talent, Formula 2 was the one vital link by which the Formula 3 hero could bridge the daunting chasm which separated him from the World Championship trail. To the ambitious Formula 3 driver, Formula 2 wasn't just important - it was essential.

Up until the end of 1970, Formula 3 provided for highly tuned 1-litre single-seaters, leaving a huge gap to the 450 brakehorsepower offered by a Cosworth DFV engined Grand Prix machine. To make that enormous transition in one jump would be as difficult as it would be imprudent. Weighing in with a capacity limit of 1.6 litres, and having readily available and servicable engines available to private customers in the form of Cosworth's FVA unit, Formula 2 offered highly competitive racing with somewhere around 220 brakehorsepower ... And there was always that tantalising prospect of 'mixing it' with established Grand Prix drivers, many of whom competed regularly in Formula 2 cars.

After his two tastes of Formula 2 in 1969, it had become quite clear that Ronnie would have little difficulty coming to terms with a paltry 220 brakehorsepower. Once his signature was dry on March's contract for 1970, Rees and Mosley got busy setting up a works Formula 2 team to contest the European Formula 2 Trophy, as it then was. Intent on ensuring that 'their' driver would have a full season in F2, whether or not they ran into any problems with his Formula 1 car, March forged a deal with a likeable F2 privateer to run their cars.

The driver involved was Malcolm Guthrie, an outspoken Worcestershireman with a cheerful vocabulary about as colourful as Ronnie's driving style. His father, Sir Giles, used to be Chairman of BOAC before retiring to the Channel Islands and the spontaneity with which his son acquired Lamborghini sports cars was indicative of the family's wealth. In 1970 the irrepressible 'Guthers' had campaigned a private Brabham BT30 and made quite a respectable job of it as well. Now he took over a financial stake in March's Formula 2 team. It turned out to be a turbulent year!

RONNIE PETERSON

The March 702, a bulky spaceframe affair, was not a success. True, Swiss privateer Xavier Perrot scored a lucky win at the poorly subscribed Nurburgring F2 race held on the same day as the temporarily exiled German Grand Prix at Hockenheim. But generally speaking, it wasn't much good. And Ronnie responded, frustrated at the car's lack of flair, by indulging in more than his fair share of crashing.

"Yer actual ace has done it again" shrugged Guthrie as a telephone message was relayed to him in the pits at Nurburgring. Ronnie had 'parked' his maroon and silver March against a barrier rather hard, so he was phoning in to see if anyone could give him a lift home!

John Watson's Brabham helps Ronnie's March off onto a trip into the unyielding sleepers at Crystal Palace in 1970

At Crystal Palace John Watson inadvertently pushed him into the sleepers. At Paul Ricard he knocked off the 702's nose section. At Rouen, a fast circuit on which the 702 seemed peculiarly at home, he was leading Siffert, Fittipaldi and Regazzoni. Until, that is, he overdid things under braking for the cobbled Nouveau Monde hairpin on the last lap and dropped to sixth. Only in the last two races of the year - at Imola and Hockenheim - did the car begin to look truly competitive and then only after extensive suspension modifications had been effected. At Hockenheim, last race of the year, Ronnie beat Emerson Fittipaldi's Lotus 69 on the very last lap to finish fourth. A portent, perhaps, of things to come.

"It might have been a bad car" remarked Robin Herd "But there's no doubt that it improved". True enough, but the painstaking and prompt development of its successor, the 712M, emphasised how conscious the March directors were about the 702's shortcomings. In 1971 they aimed not only to carry Ronnie to the European Trophy, but keep faith with the many customers they had amassed in 1970.

It was high powered stuff. For those who couldn't afford to buy and run their cars, Mosley offered 'rentadrive' arrangements whereby March provided engines and chassis for certain approved candidates to use throughout the year. At the time a lot of people complained loudly when engines became a little tired and chassis were swapped around in a complicated paddock variation of musical chairs. At £8,500 a time, these drives must have been the bargain basement of the decade. It may not have been Avis, but they certainly tried hard.

Mosley resented any suggestion that these extra drivers were helping to finance Ronnie's works car. At that price there wasn't any surplus cash left and those other cars always turned up at every race. Some financial assistance stemmed from Ronnie's Scandinavian sponsors, SMOG, but that works 712M was financed by the factory. And it repaid them admirably.

It's already been recounted how Ronnie bowed spectacularly out of his first race in the 712M - in a shower of glassfibre and mud over the bank at the Mallory Park Esses. A handful of spectators, including a little boy, suffered some minor cuts from flying debris, so Ronnie thoughtfully autographed one of the ripped front spoilers from his wrecked car and sent it along to the child as a souvenir. The race was won, ironically, by another March driven by Frenchman Henri Pescarolo from Gerry Birrell's Lotus 69 and Brian Hart, the engine wizard who prepared Peterson's FVA, in a private Brabham.

On reflection, the 1971 Formula 2 season was a vintage year. Not only was Ronnie representing the works March team but the works backed Rondel Racing Brabham team had a brace of immaculately prepared cars for Tim Schenken and Graham Hill; the works Tecnos were handled by Francois Cevert, Patrick Depailler and Jean-Pierre Jabouille; a Team Bardahl Lotus 69 was used by Emerson Fittipaldi and a similar, although slightly older machine appeared for his brother Wilson; Frank Williams had Marchs for Pescarolo and Derek Bell. Therefore, if Ronnie was to prove himself conclusively in 1971 he had the chance of doing so against the best opposition that he could ever expect to find at this level. It seemed a daunting task for March to achieve.

Even as the bits of broken March were being dug out of the bank at Mallory Park and Ronnie nursed his bruised hand back in the paddock, the problems of a multi-car works assisted team were becoming quite clear. Brian Hart, wandering round the paddock shortly before the start of the race, happened to notice the engine number of the FVA motor installed in Peterson's March. Sure enough, thought Hart, it's one of my engines. But there was something about it which rather concerned the Harlow engine builder and he quickly found Mosley and inquired just why a top line engine ordered for one of March's other 'deals' had been installed in a works car. "Don't worry" Brian was told "it'll all be alright". History unfortunately relates that it wasn't! As Ronnie lay beneath that shattered March, his foot was well and truly jammed down on the throttle pedal. The much-abused FVA, lying upside down in the frame anyway, didn't take too kindly to being over-revved in this inelegant fashion. Brian subsequently had a good deal of work to carry out on that motor before it was raceworthy again!

But this was a minor tribulation which Mosley successfully explained away later. I'd have been surprised if he'd failed to do so. Later in the year there were one or two amusing incidents when one driver 'borrowed' another driver's car for such-and-such a race because the number one driver was busy competing in another class of racing. Unfortunately the plot became rather complicated when the sponsor of the absent driver turned up at the circuit involved and discovered that 'his' driver's car was being driven by a total stranger. But, as March correctly pointed out, the arrangement was for the driver involved to have a regular drive during the year in a specific number of races. Quite what March did with the cars in the meantime shouldn't have worried the customer in the least!

At Mallory Park Ronnie proved himself to be the most competitive, and certainly the bravest, driver in Formula 2. But whilst the margin between being brilliant and actually bringing home the results is so small as to be almost immeasurable, that small chasm proved terribly frustrating and difficult for Ronnie to bridge. Once he'd done so, once the breakthrough had been successfully achieved, there was no stopping him. It was exactly the same problem facing him in Formula 1 as well.

Hockenheim, that ultra-fast German circuit near Frankfurt, was the scene of Ronnie's first Championship Formula 2 event in 1971. A spectacular infield area bounded by massive grandstands accommodating over 60,000 paying spectators is linked by a once flat-out loop rushing away into the tall pine forests and returning, equally quickly, at the opposite end of the stadium. I say 'once flat-out' because the two long straights leading away

Ronnie confers with team manager Peter Briggs prior to the start of the 1971 season's first Formula 2 Championship race at Hockenheim

from the back to the stadium now feature chicanes to lower the speed of the cars. That particular development is a direct result of an accident which took place on April 8th 1968, one which cost the life of another great driver, Jim Clark. Whilst it slows the cars down, certainly, in no way does it detract from the demanding nature of the Hockenheim circuit.

It wasn't to be Ronnie's day at the German track. Cevert's Tecno, powered by a specially developed version of the FVA motor, proved easily capable of outstripping the March on sheer speed. Ronnie finished second in one heat, but failed to complete the second owing to clutch trouble. Graham Hill, driving with a newly found lease of life for the first time since his near-fatal accident at Watkins Glen eighteen months earlier, staggered everyone by finishing second. That was the first round of the European Formula 2 Championship completed.

RONNIE PETERSON

One week after Hockenheim came the Easter Monday Thruxton meeting, a feast of speed organised regularly by the British Automobile Racing Club and a star attraction on the British racing calendar. With the great Jochen Rindt having died at Monza the previous September, the mantle of Formula 2 king had yet to be taken up by a successor to the Austrian. As everyone assembled at Thruxton for practice, it seemed impossible to believe that only a year earlier Jochen had been alive and scored one of his greatest victories at the same track. In his own Lotus 69 he'd trounced Jackie Stewart in a repeat version of his 1969 victory. Stewart may have been the race winner in Formula 1, but everybody feared Rindt in Formula 2.

By the end of 1970 there was speculation that Clay Regazzoni, the new European Formula 2 Champion, might take over the role of Formula 2 king. But Clay, good though he undoubtedly was, never looked in the position to achieve that sort of dominance, even with the clearly superior power of the works Tecno. What the fans were looking for was the instant flair, the almost uninhibited *brio,* which Rindt put into his driving. And the 1971 Thruxton race was to indicate that Ronnie could be that man.

It seems difficult to credit, even looking back four years later, that Peterson didn't win that race. Graham Hill's Brabham stormed into an immediate lead at the start of the final only for Ronnie to take up his pursuit within a couple of laps. There's no doubt that Hill was driving brilliantly, but Ronnie had his measure and chose to wait late into the race before making his move. Once it came there was no ambiguity about it, no half-heartedness. With only four laps left to go, he sliced inside Hill's blue car as they braked for the Club Chicane and emerged from the corner firmly in the lead. There was plenty of traffic on the circuit, so Hill hung on gamely and watched for every gap for an opportunity to re-pass. But it seemed that Ronnie had the strength and ability to stay ahead.

Then, with just over a lap to go, the incredible incident occurred. On the flat out right hand swerve which brings the cars back up to the hill approaching the chicane, Ronnie and Graham came upon Essex farmer Jeremy Richardson in his orange Brabham BT30. Richardson, taking things carefully in his newly acquired machine, was a novice to the formula and intent on keeping out of the way of faster cars. As the two leaders came up behind him he checked his mirrors. Marshals energetically waved a blue flag at him to indicate that he was about to be passed by some quicker competitors. Sticking firmly to the rules, Richardson checked his mirrors again on the right, saw Hill's Brabham and religiously pulled over the outside of the corner to let the Londoner pass. What he didn't realise, though, was that Ronnie had decided to pass him on the outside and, by pulling over for Graham, he'd inadvertently obliged Ronnie to take to the grass at around 140 mph!

Hill rushed through to recover his lead as Ronnie, inwardly cursing everyone and everything, wrestled to sort out the ensuing moment. He didn't have time even to shake a fist at poor Richardson and eventually regained the prescribed route successfully a little way further up the track. But it was too late to do anything more about Hill. All the way round that final lap the crowd threw hats and programmes into the air in a burst of untypically British extrovert enthusiasm, a measure of the esteem in which Graham Hill is held by the majority of race goers. But it was second place again for Ronnie ... and it began to look as though he'd attracted some dreadful jinx especially for Formula 2.

The whole affair snowballed from that point onwards. In the non-Championship Eifelrennen at the Nurburgring, Ronnie was sitting comfortably in third place behind Bell's March and Cevert's Tecno when Derek suddenly slowed as the needle of his oil pressure gauge sank ominously. As Bell eased off, Cevert swerved to one side of the circuit to avoid him. Ronnie, momentarily confused by the cloud of dust thrown up by the Tecno's rear wheels as it ran onto the sandy track border, pulled over as well. Unfortunately he just glanced the guard rail as he did so, cracking a rear wheel rim and thus allowing all the air in the tyre to escape. With over ten miles back to the pits, there was no point in his continuing, so Ronnie came sadly back to the paddock where he told Robin Herd the sad tale. Herd, by nature not easily flustered and not one to lose his bland non-commital smile in the face of disaster, grimaced. "What the hell more can we do?" he asked to anyone who would listen.

"It's ridiculous" Alan Rees would say when he was told of Ronnie's misfortunes. "He should be walking every race by a lap, but nothing's happening. Formula 2 is just pocket money to most Grand Prix drivers". Rees spoke from a position of authority. Not only was he responsible for March's success as a racing team rather than a commercial enterprise, but his experience behind the wheel proved invaluable when it came to analysing what was wrong with their Formula 2 set-up. But each time the March team broke down the component parts and took a close look, they always came back to the same conclusion. There was nothing, absolutely nothing, wrong with their team. They'd got the best driver, the best car and the best equipment. But they still weren't winning any races. It was 100 per cent, sheer undiluted frustration which prevailed at Bicester during those early summer months in 1971.

Rees went to the next Formula 2 race with Ronnie to see what was happening. It wasn't a Championship race, but the demanding prestige race round the picturesque streets of Pau, the colourful town in South West France. In many ways very similar to Monaco, and in many ways more demanding for a driver, one entrant was heard to remark of Pau "If the drivers' wives preferred Pau to Monte Carlo, then they'd run a Grand Prix here instead". Everyone laughed. Not quite accurate perhaps, but the point was taken.

Ronnie viewed the Pau race with an overwhelming feeling of

depression. Not one usually to let events get on top of him, Ronnie by now was very fed up indeed. And once again, the race turned out to be the same old format. Sure enough, Ronnie led for the first few laps. Then his March began jumping out of gear and eventually it became clear that something was going radically wrong with the chassis. With only a handful of laps completed, a disgusted Peterson came into the pits and retired. The fact that Cevert's Tecno retired at virtually the same time with a blown up engine provided little or no solace for Ronnie at all. The race was eventually won by none other than his old rival Reine Wisell, 'the other Swede', driving a Lotus 69 entered by London International Racing Associates. March team manager Pete Briggs recalls this irking Ronnie very badly.

From Pau the Formula 2 trail meandered down to Jarama in Spain, the rather uninspiring Madrid circuit being the venue for the third round of the Championship. Nursing a headache from his spectacular Silverstone accident the previous weekend, Ronnie contested the lead at Jarama with Tim Schenken's Brabham. Just 14 laps of the race had been completed when Tim came through alone. I was standing in the March pit at the time and just registered that Schenken was on his own when Ronnie appeared in the pit lane at high speed.

He overshot his pit with all four wheels locked up, slammed the March into reverse and gave it a bootfull of revs to get back to his intended point of arrival. Hardly had he stopped than he threw the safety belts off and leapt from the car. His mechanic Keith Leighton looked carefully at the engine. One of the intake trumpets was coated with petrol-soaked iron filings - another of Brian Hart's top class engines had been ruined. The weather was dull, overcast and threatening thunder, adequately reflecting the mood of the whole March team at that time. This was, without doubt, the lowest point of Ronnie's Formula 2 year. He looked about ready to scream.

A slightly incorrect suspension adjustment, made shortly before the start of the final at Crystal Palace accounted for Ronnie's spectacular third place in the popular Spring Bank Holiday Monday meeting at the colourful London circuit in a race won by his old rival Emerson Fittipaldi. With that fine Monaco second place in the bag the next port of call for his Formula 2 programme was Rouen, that classic Normandy road circuit on which he'd oh-so-nearly got it all right for Malcolm Guthrie one year earlier. Somehow one felt that this would make or break March's Formula 2 effort. If they didn't make their break through at the Rouen race, one felt, they might as well forget it all.

Ronnie's parents came to watch their son at Rouen. Ronnie's own March was prepared with more than usual diligence. Brian Hart arrived in a smart red Ferrari Dino, outwardly trying to be his normal casual self, but failing to conceal his nervousness which he shared with the usually calm Alan Rees. "We've put more effort into this race than any other" Rees told me "we're absolutely sick of losing".

Crystal Palace again, racing with Tim Schenken again, but this time in Formula 2. Ronnie's works March leads Tim's Rondel Racing Brabham BT36 during the 1971 Spring Bank Holiday International meeting. The race was won in convincing style by Emerson Fittipaldi's Lotus 69 and Tim beat Ronnie in the tussle for 2nd place

In the preliminary heat, Niki Lauda actually overtook Ronnie as they rushed down the hill to Nouveau Monde hairpin and appeared at the end of that lap just ahead of the Swede. Alan Rees nearly fell out of his pit signalling for Niki to get back behind his team leader. Ronnie wasn't too worried about Niki's ambitious plans; he knew full well that it was the final which counted. Anyway, he was impressed with his youthful Austrian friend. He later said that he realised that Niki would make a very fine Formula 1 driver, a prediction made against the general consensus of opinion at that time. Two years later, Ronnie was to be proved absolutely correct.

77

During practice at Rouen, Ronnie gave Niki Lauda a lift back to the pits after his car had broken down on the circuit. Here the Austrian balances precariously on the engine cover of the March as they arrive in the pit lane

The thing that one always remembers about Rouen is the ambiance, the pleasantly informal atmosphere. But it was lost on the March team in 1971. They were looking down a narrow corridor towards that first Formula 2 victory for the works team. All outside considerations and influences had been blanked out completely. Although Ronnie maintained an outward air of casual indifference, this simply smothered that overwhelming desire to succeed. He'd seen men distinctly less capable than himself winning Formula 2 races. He was tired of that. Now he dearly wanted, no needed, some victory for himself.

It was an easier race than the March team could ever have expected. Cevert's Tecno, Ronnie's big rival, spun into a barrier early in the race, leaving Ronnie well ahead. The March crew couldn't believe it. Ronnie was lapping alone, under no pressure. He began to hear noises from the engine, noises which were not there at all. He began to imagine the clutch playing up, the brakes feeling spongy. No, there was nothing. In the pits his parents waited with Barbro. Rees tutored him diligently with pit signals. There was almost heart-stopping concern as his lap times lengthened. No, there was no hint of trouble. Rees was just pacing him as slowly as he dared. 'EZE' said the boards as Ronnie reeled off those final precious laps. Time seemed to stand still; would he never appear. Then it was all over. The chequered flag fluttered, Ronnie's arm raised high in the air and the yellow March was on its slowing down lap. Then the unbridled sense of relief mingled with happiness engulfed the whole team. They didn't know whether to laugh or cry with delight. The break through had been achieved at last!

The sweet moment of triumph - swinging his March through Rouen's Nouveau Monde hairpin on his way to that first, elusive Formula 2 win - June, 1971

RONNIE PETERSON

Once Ronnie had won his first long-awaited Formula 2 victory, the others seemed to follow like a flood. At Mantorp Park and Karlskoga, Ronnie became a hero on his home soil. At Brands Hatch on August Bank Holiday Monday his fastest lap was within a few tenths of the outright Formula 1 record. He took the lead round the outside of South Bank. People don't do things like that, but Ronnie did. He slayed the opposition. While he was running, the others were genuinely racing for second place. With success he tended to relax slightly, he wasn't so tensed up. That enabled him to achieve even more success. At Tulln-Langenlebarn, a dismal and bleak airfield circuit near Vienna, he so utterly dominated the race in such pouring rain that his pit hung out a signal saying 'REGN' - meaning rain - just in case he hadn't noticed the conditions! As far as Ronnie was concerned, the track might have been bone dry.

The night after that race, Ronnie seemed just a little bit on the quiet side. A group of us went to a typical Vienna beer cellar to celebrate. Niki Lauda and his girlfriend Mariella were there with Francois Cevert and his girlfriend Christina, Austrian journalist Heinz Prueller, Ronnie, Barbro and myself. Lauda drove a borrowed BMW 2002 through the soaking streets of Vienna with a brand of panache which left me shaking for about an hour. "He'll be alright" I told Ronnie "if he lives long enough. He's a bloody lunatic on the road". Ronnie smiled. His own style of driving wasn't terribly different and he drove a V8 Mercedes. I decided I was glad I'd driven with Niki.

By the end of the evening, Francois Cevert was dominating the proceedings. A complete contrast to Ronnie, Francois was an extrovert of the first order and he had the charm and looks to carry it off as well. His tap dancing on the table top was so popular with the other occupants of the cellar that the owner declined to intervene and allowed the handsome Frenchman to monopolise everyone's attention until the small hours. Ronnie simply sat and thought, probably about the European Championship victory which was now well within his capabilities. But he still had to beat Cevert as well as Carlos Reutemann, the dusky Argentinian who drove a Brabham financed partly by the Argentinian Government.

Emerson Fittipaldi, himself not eligible for European Championship points owing to his Grand Prix success the previous year, won the penultimate race of the season at Albi in South West France. Ronnie finished fifth, but to this day there is some argument as to whether March contravened the regulations by adding oil during a pit stop. I watched the car glide to a halt just in front of me and I certainly wouldn't like to be called on to make a definite judgement on the matter. One way or another, nobody raised any embarrassing questions once the chequered flag had fallen, so Ronnie retained his hard earned position. Then came the pinnacle of March's achievement; Vallelunga.

Rome's Vallelunga circuit is neatly laid out but proves quite

Max Mosley (left) and Alan Rees greet Peterson as he lifts himself from his March after setting the fastest practice time at Brands Hatch. August Bank Holiday Saturday, 1971

Argued by many to be his finest Formula 2 victory, Ronnie's win at Brands Hatch on August Bank
Holiday Monday, 1971, was brilliant. He lapped almost on the Formula 1 record with his Formula 2
March and never looked in the least flustered

Watching that sensational performance at Brands Hatch, the F2 March crew crowd against the pit
wall as Ronnie speeds on towards victory. Robin Herd is the one in the STP jacket

One of Ronnie's best wet-weather performances came at the bleak Tulln-Langenlebarn airfield near Vienna in September 1971. With the track circuit absolutely swimming in water, he held off Tim Schenken's Brabham BT36 for another fine win of a memorable season

'RONNIE - RAIN' says the tongue-in-cheek sign hung out to SuperSwede by March's Peter Briggs at Tulln Langenlebarn. It didn't seem to affect Ronnie's performance in any way as he speedboated to his fifth Formula 2 win of the season

demanding to drive quickly. Somewhat on the narrow side, it poses problems for overtaking and inevitably offers close and exciting competition. For Ronnie Peterson, it was the scene of his European Championship triumph in October 1971. The weather was perfect; not a single cloud could be seen in the deep blue sky. In fact it was so hot that some doubt existed as to whether the soft compound slick tyres would last the required distance. It was a worry which prompted Reutemann's team manager to opt for harder compound, grooved covers for the Argentinian's Brabham, a decision which virtually lost him all reasonable chance of taking on Peterson in a straight fight.

Once Emerson Fittipaldi's Lotus retired with a broken throttle cable on the third lap, Ronnie was left alone to speed his way to victory. Although the March camp was pretty well used to the taste of victory by this stage in the season, Vallelunga was something different. This was the very peak of their achievement, something on which they would look back on with fond memories for many years to come. When the chequered flag finally fell at the Roman circuit, Ronnie was European Champion. It was a deeply moving experience.

Unfortunately the joy of the moment wasn't something that Ronnie could stop and savour. He was scheduled to drive Jo Bonnier's Lola sports car at Barcelona the following day, so he ran hand in hand with Barbro to a waiting Carabinieri helicopter standing on the infield ready to whisk him across the Rome airport and the evening scheduled flight to Spain. Still wearing his overalls, he gave Barbro a quick kiss on the cheek in front of the gaping onlookers and leapt into the helicopter. A final fleeting wave to the happy throng and he was gone, leaving the March team to celebrate loud and long into the night. And celebrate they did. Monday morning saw most of the deck chairs at the Bela Motel decanted into the swimming pool as well as a lot of people nursing the worst hangovers of their life.

"There were too many cars. There were not enough engines". Ronnie was right when he pointed these facts out. But, by and large, he admitted that 1971 was a good Formula 2 year. The right man won the Championship, he won it convincingly and he won it against top flight opposition. At the end of 1971, Formula 2 changed its regulations to accommodate 2-litre motors derived from production-based engines. These were regulations which eventually caused a lot of expense and anguish for many engine builders and ensured that Formula 2 took a full two years to return to the level of competitiveness which it sustained in 1971. Some say it never did return to that level, but personal memories are always coloured by personal involvement and are frequently unreliable when recalling facts. But for me Formula 2 never subsequently quite achieved that fine, fine edge of competition which was its hallmark throughout 1971. By any standards it was a memorable year.

Brian Hart in consultation with Ronnie at Vallelunga. Hart's Harlow firm prepared the Cosworth FVA motors which March fitted to Peterson's car during his 1971 Formula 2 Championship season

In front again. Ronnie leads Emerson Fittipaldi's Lotus 69 in the final round of the European Formula 2 Championship at Vallelunga, near Rome in October 1971. Fittipaldi dropped out after a couple of laps when his Lotus' throttle cable broke, leaving Peterson to drive on to his sixth victory of the season and his long-awaited title

Rees shares a problem with Ronnie. The little Welshman was on hand to watch Ronnie win his European crown at Vallelunga and, three years later, tried hard to woo the Swede away from Lotus and into the UOP Shadow Grand Prix team

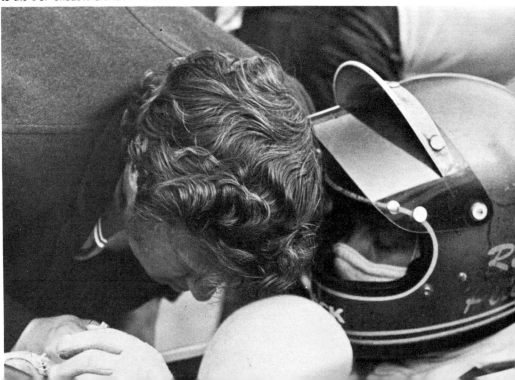

With one front wheel cocked nearly over a kerb in a tight Vallelunga hairpin, Peterson powers onwards to victory. He departed before victory celebrations to fly to Barcelona for a sports car event the following day. He won that as well!

Although Ronnie has never appeared to change with his increasing success as a racing driver, his European Championship victory left him a far more assured performer. Just like Rindt, Peterson needed his Formula 2 success as a substitute for Grand Prix victories. Just as Rindt had battled from 1965 to 1969 with uncompetitive Formula 1 cars, so he achieved all the more with his Formula 2 machinery. When Grand Prix success came his way Rindt no longer <u>needed</u> to do well in Formula 2. With Peterson the transition was slightly different. He still had another year contracted to March at the time he won his European Championship victory so the appeal of Formula 2 success was not completely diluted in 1972.

In fact, March started off 1972 looking as well prepared as just about anyone. Ronnie rather blotted his copybook at the freezing March Mallory meeting by creaming his new 722 into the barrier at Gerards Corner - the opposite end of the circuit to his shunt of the previous year! Niki Lauda newly recruited into the March works team for both Formula 1 and Formula 2, saved the day for March by finishing second.

RONNIE PETERSON

Easter Monday Thruxton enabled Ronnie to avenge his previous season's bad luck and he won the race in dominating style, leading team mates Cevert and Lauda for a crushing Bicester 1–2–3 triumph. But away from Grand Prix racing, Ronnie had another commitment in 1972 apart from Formula 2. He was now a member of the all-conquering Ferrari sports car team and, at the wheel of a 3-litre flat-12 312P, had already won the Buenos Aires 1000 Kilometres race with Tim Schenken. Ronnie by now had decided that the tang of success was something he could usefully acquire a taste for. He didn't take in a great number of Formula 2 races in 1972 as a result, although when he did compete, he was generally a man to be reckoned with.

Whilst the second half of 1972 was taken up with those complicated discussions as to whether or not he'd be joining Lotus for the following season, Ronnie managed to retain his interest in Formula 2. At the final John Player Championship round at Oulton Park, Ronnie won the race from team mate Lauda by a matter of feet. Even then nobody seemed unduly convinced about Niki's ability. "I'm telling you, he's good" reaffirmed Ronnie after that race, even though matters rather more weighty than the pros and cons of Niki's driving prowess were well to the forefront of his mind. Within a few weeks, the decision was irrevocable. Ronnie would be driving for Lotus in 1973, whatever anyone said, thought or did.

During the winter he accepted an invitation to drive for the very competitive Motul-Rondel Formula 2 team in the three race Brazilian Torneio series, races hardly blessed with good results for the cheerful Swede. But Ronnie was relaxed by now, he seemed to have discovered himself insofar as he now knew how good he was. Inwardly he'd always suspected that the ability to compete with the best was always lurking. He'd never doubted that. Now the offer from Lotus and his acceptance meant that he would have the opportunity to win Grand Prix motor races the following year. Of that there was little doubt. To add to Ronnie's confidence and sense of security over his move to Team Lotus, Keith Leighton followed Super-swede to Hethel. Keith had moved to the highly professional Rondel team after that successful 1971 European Championship season and was more than keen to accept Ronnie's invitation to follow him. For over two years now, Keith has tended to Ronnie's Formula 1 Lotus with a singlemindedness which fully justifies Ronnie's enormous faith in his ability.

That Lotus contract virtually debarred him from driving for another team, so he was unable to commit himself to a second season of sports cars with Ferrari. But Colin Chapman, enterprising as usual, had another project in the pipeline to keep his drivers occupied when they were not driving in Grand Prix events. He'd just recruited a new designer, former Brabham and McLaren man Ralph Bellamy, and this quiet Australian's first task was to build a Formula 2 chassis to take a racing version of the new 2-litre Lotus which had been produced for the Jensen Healey sports car. The motor was to be race prepared by Novamotor, the Italian specialists who had done such

Three-wheeling in style, Peterson's March 722 lifts a wheel as he speeds to victory at Thruxton on Easter Monday 1972. He was never challenged from the start, leading Francois Cevert and Niki Lauda across the line in a triumphant 1-2-3 finish for March

Deep in conversation with Goodyear's Ed Alexander prior to a Grand Prix

a good job on Ronnie's Formula 3 motors four years earlier. Bellamy's design was strikingly Lotus, the cars employing inboard brakes all round as well as torsion bar suspension. Soon it became clear that the Lotus 73s were a 'dummy run' in preparation for a brand new Grand Prix chassis in 1974. And that would be the ill-fated Lotus 76.

The Lotus 73s were eventually sponsored by Texaco and known as Texaco Stars in much the same way as the works Formula 1 cars were John Player Specials. Testing wasn't too encouraging and the brutal truth became realised once the cars got to compete in races. They weren't fast enough. One or two people in the Lotus hierachy seemed rather resentful that the engines should have been prepared by Novamotor. It was felt, fairly confidently in some quarters, that the factory could make a better job of things and develop substantially more power than Novamotor. One way or another, the commitment had been made and Lotus were now pledged to see the season out. Emerson Fittipaldi made it pretty plain that he couldn't care in the slightest about the Texaco Star and the cars didn't get to very many races anyway. Peter Warr's hopes about fielding the reigning World Champion and the fastest driver in the world, side by side in the same team, didn't exactly come to fruition. Basically that was the car's fault, not the drivers'.

Although he regularly drove anything he was given flat out, Ronnie didn't seem desperately concerned whether he drove the Texaco Star or not. He had a nasty fright in one at Rouen, coming within inches of an extremely unpleasant accident in the process. Just after the first flat out kink beyond the pits, the organisers erected a polystyrene bale chicane following practice after consultation with the drivers. This was the ill-conceived backlash of a fatal accident to the popular Scottish driver Gerry Birrell who had been killed on Saturday when his works Chevron crashed into the guard rail further down the hill towards Nouveau Monde. The reasoning behind the apparently inexplicable siting of this chicane was that it would slow cars down from the dangerous speeds which were being attained further down the hill, at the point where Birrell's crash occurred.

The logic behind the decision was totally confused. Nevertheless, Ronnie raced with everyone else, whirling the Texaco Star round a great deal quicker than anyone thought it was capable of going. He established the fastest lap in his heat and finished fourth. In the final he was running mid-field when he clipped a front wheel against that chicane on one near-fateful lap. Almost unbelievably, the impact damaged the steering rack, allowing the teeth to jump and leaving the bewildered Swede with no means of guiding his car. It charged the guard rail, slithered crazily along the top for many yards and then crashed down on the sandy track border. Ronnie erupted from the cockpit like a missile, stalking back up the hill towards the pits with a look of thunder on his face. Team manager Jim Endruwit was very concerned about the whole affair. It wasn't necessary for Ronnie to make any comment at all.

He drove the car again that summer, but his enthusiasm for it was never terribly conspicuous. Nevertheless, his Formula 1 score was at last off the ground. By the time he appeared at the ultra-fast Enna-Pergusa circuit in Sicily to drive the Texaco Star at the end of August, he'd already won the French and Austrian Grands Prix. A totally different Ronnie emerged at last. No longer really bothered whether the Formula 2 car went well or not, there was no sign of annoyance when he discovered that the steering column was a bit on the loose side. He beamed happily when he recounted how he'd glanced the guard rail at around 160 mph.

He could at last see the amusing side of his misfortunes. It wasn't a question of coming to terms with them though, he'd been obliged to do that too frequently over the past three seasons. Now he had reached the sport's highest level - he was a Grand Prix winner. In Enna he laughed and joked casually, that bright smile became familiar again. He laughed loudly and frequently and thoroughly enjoyed the elaborate victory celebrations and presentation which took place in the open courtyard beneath the castle walls at the top of the town.

The next morning he proved absolutely irrepressible on the auto-strada back to Palermo airport. Slipstreaming like Mike Hailwood and Carlos Pace proved a necessarily dubious affair in Fiat 128s and I was lucky that my 2.6 litre German built Ford Granada had the edge on them when it came to sheer speed. I soon realised the trick was *not* to lead the bunch because neither of them would then allow me to drop back behind. They simply ran side by side, forcing whoever was leading to keep the speed up as high as they thought prudent!

Once we boarded the Alitalia DC-9 for the flight to London via Genoa, Ronnie became really mischievous. Mike Hailwood tried desperately to read his current paper back despite continual harrassment from his Swedish colleague. Once Ronnie tired of trying to disrupt Mike's attention he inadvertently found himself dismantling the snap-down tray on the back

His Texaco Star is just about to collide with the barrier during the 1973 Rouen Formula 2 Race

of the seat in front of him. Mike decided that he'd best take an interest in whatever Ronnie was doing lest he turn his attention to the emergency exit sign which hung next to Ronnie's seat. From that point onwards the flight was complete and utter chaos, Ronnie crowning it all by loading all the rubbish off his lunch tray into a plastic glass before crushing it all over Mike's lap. Ronnie could be like that sometimes!

The end of 1973 virtually spelt the end of Ronnie Peterson Formula 2 driver. In the four seasons during which he'd been a regular competitor, his trade mark had become driving spectacle and his value the same one hundred per cent effort which he always applied to his Formula 1 driving. In proving that he had the necessary ability to graduate to Grand Prix racing, Ronnie himself became the standpoint he himself was aiming for. He'd come in trying to match the best and ended up being the one by which others measured their own performances. Even in a totally uncompetitive car, Ronnie could be relied upon to appear unusually close to the front of the field.

At the end of the 1973 season, Lotus abandoned the Texaco Star project completely and their Formula 2 team was disbanded. That meant that any races Ronnie might compete in outside Formula 1 were limited to a commitment with the works BMW saloon team. Needless to say his progress in a 3.4 litre CSL from Munich was as fast and spectacular as one would have expected. History does relate that he managed to write one off during a national saloon race in his native Sweden - Ronnie keeps rather quiet on that subject! But he also managed to smash one of the works cars into the back of an errant sports car during the Kyalami 9 Hour race at the end of 1974. What that story does conceal however is that Ronnie in a works BMW saloon was quite simply the fastest thing round the Kyalami track during the race's rain-soaked early stages.

Later, as he grappled with Formula 1 throughout 1975, both March directors wanted dearly to get him back into one of their Formula 2 cars. Their highly productive link with BMW for the provision of 2-litre engines had meant that their cars were virtually invincible during 1973 and 1974. Now they wanted to solve that tantalising problem. How would Ronnie go in a March BMW? They eventually persuaded Lotus to permit him a run at Karlskoga, in front of his home crowd. He caught and passed the 1974 European Champion elect Patrick Depailler, the Frenchman driving a similar works car, and won the race.

Depailler clearly allowed Peterson to take the lead, knowing full-well that there was a maximum helping of Championship points waiting for him whether he beat Ronnie or not. The thing many people might have been keen to watch would have been Depailler making genuine efforts to stay in front of Ronnie. Had he done so, then there's very little doubt as to the race's outcome. Ronnie would have won anyway. He was still a genuine King of Formula 2.

Bouncing a wheel over the chicane kerb at Thruxton, Easter Monday 1975. A few laps later Ronnie's March-BMW collided with a slower car at the same place, triggering off a multi-car pile-up

Clinching the deal? Ronnie shakes hands with Peter Warr at the Lotus factory after signing his two year contract to drive for Chapman's team at the end of the 1972 season

CHAPTER 4
The lure of Lotus

THAT RONNIE PETERSON would eventually drive for Team Lotus at some time in his career, seems to have been inevitable. One of Ronnie's few positive aspirations was to drive for Colin Chapman and the reasoning behind that ambition was quite clear. Chapman's Lotus Grand Prix cars have provided a World Champion driver with his mount for five of the past eleven years. On each occasion Lotus cars won the Constructors Championship and, in 1973, they won it again although neither of their drivers was World Champion.

Colin Chapman is one of the few people in modern day motor racing which the word 'brilliant' can be used truthfully to describe. The rise of his Lotus organisation from humble beginnings in a back street garage in suburban Hornsey to a multi-million pound firm based at a spacious, modern factory in Norfolk, spanned a mere sixteen years. In motor racing he has been an innovator, trend setter and the man who sets the pace. Others follow paths hewn by Chapman's shrewd judgement and intuitive feeling for racing cars and the people who drive them.

Hand in hand with the success, Chapman has experienced more than his fair share of tragedy. Jim Clark, the brilliant Scottish driver with whom Chapman won two World Championships plus the Indianapolis 500, was killed in a minor Formula Two event in Germany at the start of 1968. Chapman bounced back, only for tragedy to repeat itself at Monza at the end of 1970. Jochen Rindt, the great Austrian star who joined Lotus at the start of 1969, died during practice for the Italian Grand Prix. Rindt became Grand Prix racing's first posthumous World Champion.

It was shortly after that shattering experience that Chapman first talked to Peterson. Ever watchful of the rising stars in Formula One, Chapman had kept a close eye on Peterson ever since his debut at Monaco. Already he'd recruited Emerson Fittipaldi as a Lotus 'coming-man', but now the prospects looked bleak. Although his team missed the Canadian Grand Prix, two Lotus 72s arrived at Watkins Glen for the United States Grand Prix, last but one event on the Championship trail.

Partnering Emerson Fittipaldi, who should be in the team but Ronnie's compatriot Reine Wisell? It's now history that, at the age of 23,

Emerson Fittipaldi became a surprised winner of his fourth ever Grand Prix after an amazing race of changing fortunes which saw Pedro Rodriguez in a BRM robbed of the chequered flag with just a few laps left to run when a pit stop for extra fuel deprived him of the lead. Reine Wisell, driving his very first Grand Prix in the second Lotus 72, took an excellent third place behind Rodriguez.

But Chapman was very definitely impressed with Peterson. He talked frankly with the March driver who was now obliged to stay another couple of seasons with March, the promoted team leader. Chris Amon and the March directors had arrived virtually at the point where no future existed for them together and Amon was on the verge of signing with the French Matra organisation. Chapman, seriously considering running Peterson in a third Lotus alongside his two contracted men, made a big effort to rustle up extra backing for 1971, but failed. And March wanted Ronnie dearly for that three year stint; Alan Rees knew who he wanted, and for how long.

At Mexico City, venue of the last Grand Prix of the year, Amon finally split with March. At last Max Mosley agreed that Ronnie would be number one driver in the STP sponsored team for 1972 and 1973. "Put it in writing" grinned Ronnie. And Mosley did just that. Team Lotus faced the 1971 with the least experienced line-up of Grand Prix drivers in the whole Formula One circus, while March came up with a brand new, semi-streamlined chassis, the 711, for Peterson and the attendant miscellany of sports car and saloon drivers which because of Mosley's dealings with Alfa Romeo, were to share the Formula 1 cars with Ronnie.

Chapman's team had an indifferent season. The nearest they came to winning a Grand Prix was in Austria where Emerson Fittipaldi was in sight of Jo Siffert's victorious BRM when the chequered flag came out. The BRM had a deflating rear tyre and probably wouldn't have managed another lap in the lead. That thought provided no solace for Chapman who was used to getting his cars into the winner's circle.

Fittipaldi had real talent, Chapman fully recognised that, and it was only a matter of time before it matured the Brazilian into a Grand Prix winner. It was hard to believe that he'd got less than a year's experience in Grand Prix racing behind him as he diced expertly with fellow newcomer Tim Schenken in the Austrian sunshine. He'd suffered a nasty road accident, in which his wife Maria-Helena sustained some unpleasant facial injuries, and his splendid third place behind the Tyrrells of Jackie Stewart and Francois Cevert in the French Grand Prix at Paul Ricard was a triumph of determination. He was driving with a badly damaged ribcage a few weeks after the road crash.

By contrast Reine Wisell was proving to be something of a disappointment to Chapman. When he was good, he was very good indeed "But he had his off-days" remarked the Lotus chief "and on those occasions he wasn't much good at all". Chapman was later to draw comparisons between the two Swedish drivers that he employed. "They had very similar approaches in many ways, but Reine was moody whereas very little upsets Ronnie. In fact that's one of Ronnie's great assets. He's phlegmatic and extremely philosophical. He always gives his best, he tries hard consistently. And that's particularly important at a test session, for example. He's always quick and he never has off-days. Therefore if he's going quickly, then you know that the car is quick, if he's going slowly then you know the car is slow. You don't have to make allowances for him like you do with other drivers as to whether or not they've got an off-day".

Wisell finally left the team at the end of the 1971 season and Emerson Fittipaldi stayed. Chapman then took one of his few gambles over drivers which failed to come off. He promoted Australian Dave Walker to the Formula 1 team alongside Fittipaldi after the previous Formula 3 season in which he'd won 25 of the 31 races in which he took part. Fittipaldi went on to become World Champion, Walker simply proved too slow.

Chapman is never one to miss an opportunity and Ronnie Peterson's impressive string of second places in the March kept the Lotus chief's eyes firmly focussed in his direction. The Swede clearly looked the fastest thing on the circuit apart from Jackie Stewart, the one star driver Chapman had endeavoured to woo and failed with. Now he dearly wanted Peterson to run alongside Fittipaldi in his cars and informal talks throughout the 1971 season with Peterson seemed to strengthen the possibility of him joining Lotus at the end of 1972.

There was plenty of chat, some serious, some not so serious, but these rumours put Max Mosley on the defensive. After all it was March Engineering who gave Ronnie his big break and, apart from trying to keep tabs on every extremity of March's fast-mushrooming business, he devoted himself with an almost passionate fervour to emphasising that Ronnie Peterson was a March contracted driver. At least until the end of 1972.

Max Mosley doesn't get ruffled easily. Nevertheless, when Alex Soler-Roig blew up one of his team's Cosworth DFV engines in the 1971 Dutch Grand Prix at Zandvoort he almost lost his diffident air of good-humoured nonchalance, and Andrea de Adamich's leisurely gait at the wheel of the March-Alfa Romeo at Silverstone the same year, left him fairly explosive. But there were few other occasions during that successful Grand Prix season when he showed anything more than mild irritation.

Except at Nurburgring, venue for the German Grand Prix Chapman jokingly remarked to Ronnie - "you'll have to drive for me or Ken (Tyrrell) in 1972, because there will be six special DFVs. Three for me and three for Ken". Mosley, by now increasingly at odds with fellow director Alan Rees over whether March was primarily a racing team or a commercial concern, probably saw the taunt as a larger than life threat to Ronnie's contract. He couldn't really believe that Keith Duckworth and Ford would administer preferential treatment to specified teams, but he wasn't one hundred percent certain.

He opted for a confrontation with Chapman. Engineering an apparently chance paddock meeting between himself, Chapman and Ford Motor Company director Walter Hayes, one of the men originally behind the £100,000 package deal which Ford forged with Cosworth Engineering for the development of that Grand Prix motor. "About those special engines, Colin ..." Max spoke with a confidence he, at least, hoped was convincing. Chapman was too wily to be hung with his own rope and laughed the matter off. Mosley subsequently wondered whether he should have mentioned it, but decided that at least everyone knew the lay of the land. Maybe he was being too sensitive.

Perhaps encouraged by Mosley's obvious sensitivity on the question of Ronnie's contract, Chapman threw another bone out in Max's direction "Tell you what, I'll give you £60,000 for the balance of Ronnie's contract". Mosley grinned "Really Colin, how's that".

"Well you'll save the £30,000 you'd have had to pay him and I'll give you Wilson Fittipaldi's contract and he'll bring along £30,000 in sponsorship". Whether the jovial suggestion finally taxed Mosley's humour to breaking point or not is hardly clear, but by the end of the weekend Chapman was completely convinced over what he already really knew.

Ronnie Peterson would stay at March Engineering for his three year stint. "It wasn't that it was simply over Ronnie", laughed Herd "but one of them had to win and one to lose. Neither Max nor Colin liked losing".

Meanwhile, Ronnie remained quite content with his lot at March. He was heading for second place in the World Championship, the 711 was quite a good car and his performances in the Italian and Canadian Grand Prixs left everyone with little doubt that he was now a driver of world class and ability. Mosley and Herd were fully aware of the increasing status of their protege, also appreciating that the 1972 Grand Prix March would have to be top class in order to have a chance of retaining Peterson in the team for 1973.

Ronnie liked the atmosphere at March and had quite a strong loyalty to the three directors, in particular Alan Rees. They in turn felt an almost protective soft spot for 'their' driver whom they'd brought up from Formula 3. Why? Once again Herd explained simply "He is just the best, the quickest and the nicest".

Meanwhile, Colin Chapman was marshalling his forces for 1972. 1971 had been an indifferent season for his team, but they received a well earned confidence booster at the end of the season. Imperial Tobacco, the holding company, who'd sponsored the Lotus Grand Prix team since the start of 1968, endorsed their faith in the Lotus team by agreeing to John Player & Son (the Nottingham based tobacco company) to sponsor them for a further three years. But the distinctive red, white and gold livery of Gold Leaf Team Lotus now changed. The cigarette which had to be promoted was now the John Player Special and the Lotus 72s assumed a slinky black and gold livery to open the 1972 season. Purists bemoaned this move, for the cars were now called John Player Specials and registered thus at the CSI where they would score World Championship points under this title. Chapman sympathised inwardly with dyed-in-the-wool enthusiasts. Having brought the name Lotus into Grand Prix racing he naturally had some regret in seeing it passing. But he recognised that Lotus itself could not sustain the ever increasing financial burden of Formula 1 on its own. Reflecting that it now cost upwards of £200,000 per year, to operate an effective two car challenge, he accepted Player's money gratefully.

Chapman's faith in Emerson Fittipaldi was certainly not misplaced confidence. Now completely recovered from the long-term effects of that road accident the young Brazilian got into his stride. The Lotus 72 chassis still proved to be a highly competitive proposition and, opening his score with a second place to Denny Hulme's McLaren M19A in the South African Grand Prix at Kyalami, he piled on the pressure in his quest for the Championship Crown.

As Ronnie quickly discovered, that novel engineering exercise, the March 721X, was nothing more than a frustrating blind alley as far as his championship aspirations were concerned. He struggled gamely with Herd's complicated concept and finally resigned himself to the fact that it was hopeless.

Emerson Fittipaldi won in Spain, Belgium, Britain, Austria and Italy to assume the World Championship laurels from Jackie Stewart's shoulders and be hailed as a worthy successor to that title.

At March it was a race against time to prove that the 721G was highly competitive. But the strenuous toil at the Bicester factory failed to make up for the time lost with the troublesome 721X. Ground lost in Grand Prix racing is virtually impossible to catch up on. Had this disaster intruded into Ronnie's 1971 season, it might have been possible to pull the whole team out of the mire and catch up time for 1972. It was to be amusing for the casual observer, and utterly galling for the March directors to see their 721G running right up with the leaders during 1973 - in the hands of a private team. James Hunt in the Hesketh March, fully sorted and developed by Harvey Postlethwaite, topped the 1972 season by finishing in second place at Watkins Glen. A few feet in front of him, scooping the 50,000 dollar treasure trove for first place came Ronnie Peterson in his JPS Lotus.

Obviously thoughts of Ronnie's potential performance in a 731, as the car was dubbed in its 1973 guise, were depressing to March's directors. Would Ronnie have stayed with March had the 721G been fully competitive from an early stage? It's a question which the Swede shies away from; "It's possible. I think I would like to have stayed with March. But, as I'd turned down an offer from Lotus, I might have regretted it for the rest of my career". Ronnie was right. He might never have been given another chance. **99**

..... and so does Colin Chapman!

At the end of August he signed an option to drive for Colin Chapman during 1973 and 74.

The motor racing press, fired by speculative fuel from non-committal March directors, went straight into top gear. Some suggested that Chapman had misinformed Ronnie as to the precise nature of the document he had signed. They suggested that Ronnie thought it was an option on his part. But it all proved to be wishful thinking. Ronnie realised full-well what he was doing. Chapman explained in some detail.

"The reason we signed Ronnie on an option basis was that, at that stage in the season, we were not fully certain that our sponsors would back us to the extent of having two number one drivers on the team. If we hadn't got Ronnie to sign that option, I might well have reached agreement with our sponsors and then found that another team had snapped him up. On the other hand I had to go to the sponsor and say 'Look, I've got a commitment with Ronnie providing we can agree terms'. That's why we signed that option with him, not to trap him but just to ensure we were on firm ground when it came to finalising the arrangement".

The contract was, of course, finalised. Now the shackles of frustration had been thrown off, Ronnie was about to enter the most successful phase of his career as a Grand Prix driver.

If Chapman is to enter two cars, he wants them both to have a strong chance of winning. He made motor racing history back in 1967 when he invited Graham Hill to leave BRM, his home for the previous eight seasons, and rejoin Lotus which he'd left in 1959. But with the backing of Ford and the new Cosworth DFV motor, Team Lotus became a devastating force to be reckoned with even though they didn't win the Championship, either championship. Hill then salvaged the title from the depths of their tragic 1968 season and, the following year, the line-up looked even more imposing with the British driver joined by Jochen Rindt and Mario Andretti.

In 1970, Rindt's brilliance in the Lotus 72 overshadowed the efforts of his number two, John Miles, but Chapman noticed that his second driver was rather less than inspired. Unfortunately for Miles, his year with the Lotus 72 came at a time when several other Grand Prix novices were showing themselves off with distinction. Then came the barren outlook after Monza. Rindt was dead and Miles retired from the team. Only Chapman could weld everything back together in time for Emerson Fittipaldi to win the United States GP at Watkins Glen. He was the youngest driver ever to achieve such a landmark, and he did it in only his fourth Grand Prix.

Then came the contrasting years of 1972 and 1973. Neither Fittipaldi nor Wisell produced any wins in 1971, but Chapman's confidence in the Brazilian never wavered in the least. He spoke enthusiastically in interviews with the press over Emerson's fantastic potential. He reaffirmed his belief that he could win the World Championship. After the greyest year from the point of view of results, in Team Lotus' history, only a minority shared this confidence. It was vindicated magnificently in 1972. The only person not surprised in the least was Colin Chapman.

But how does a driver react when he suddenly finds his domain invaded by a potentially stronger rival? This was the situation which Emerson Fittipaldi found himself facing at the end of 1972. He had just become motor racing's youngest World Champion. He was just starting to develop a smooth and stylish flair which prompted even the most seasoned journalist to liken the Brazilian to Jim Clark. His number two had never looked remotely like approaching the kind of performances that win races, never mind championships, and suddenly he was expected to receive his closest rival into the team alongside him.

Emerson reacted diplomatically. He fully realised the advances that were being made to Peterson during 1972 and fully appreciated the threat to his supremacy at Team Lotus. But Emerson and Ronnie were, and still are, close friends. Thus, while clearly being understandably cool about the whole project, Emerson Fittipaldi remained scrupulously polite towards any prying press inquiries. Polite, but inwardly cautious.

To say that the Fittipaldi-Peterson arrangement was an ideal set-up with the approval of both drivers would not be entirely true. For Fittipaldi it was an intrusion on his ground. Perhaps his Latin temperament was to magnify the problems of the following twelve months in his own eyes. Certainly, Peterson's Nordic resilience seemed to cope better with inevitable ups and downs which must strain even the most efficient operation whilst trying to operate four cars, two for each driver, to as near identical specification as humanly possible.

But, when the total of Team Lotus' efforts for 1973 were added up, Colin Chapman must have been utterly delighted. For the first time since 1958, the champion car was not driven by the Champion driver. Although Jackie Stewart wrote the finale to a successful Grand Prix career with his third title, the black and gold Lotus 72s of Peterson and Fittipaldi won seven Grand Prix races between them. More than any other marque. And Lotus emerged as Champion Car Constructors.

It proved to be a fascinating season of waxing and waning fortunes for the five drivers who blazed a trail to the Grand Prix winner's circle, but primarily it will be remembered as the year in which Ronnie Peterson finally came across the finishing line first. His three year tenure at March had labelled the blonde Swede as a perpetually unlucky exponent of his high speed art. Even when he took the step of throwing off the March shackles, which, by the end of that three years were becoming something of a handicap, he didn't achieve any instant success at Team Lotus. In fact he wasn't particularly quick in his first race at the wheel of a Lotus 72. But once he savoured victory, and proved that his terrific natural flair could be tempered with a smattering of moderation, Ronnie Peterson finally became the Grand Prix force which Alan Rees had realised he could become ever since he first

With his old friend and Ferrari team mate Tim Schenken

watched him back at Albi in 1969.

Fittipaldi wasn't about to be toppled in a few minutes. If Ronnie ended up at the finish of the 1973 season with a slight psychological advantage over the Brazilian, it was no reflection on Emerson's ability behind the wheel of a Grand Prix car. Indeed, the first two races of 1973 suggested that Emerson might devour the opposition in the same way as he had done the previous year. Under a scorching Argentinian sun, he dispatched the Tyrrells of Stewart and Cevert with a top class example of controlled aggression and waited only another two weeks before leading the Brazilian Grand Prix from start to finish in front of his home crowd. Perhaps Fittipaldi would be Champion two years running.

Ronnie might have been forgiven for being highly depressed after those first two races. His engine started seizing at Buenos Aires, forcing him to quit his first race in a Lotus 72 after 67 of the 96 laps while in Brazil. He was about to take issue with Stewart over second place when his car suddenly spun wildly out of control on one of the very fastest corners on the circuit. A wheel had broken up, so Ronnie was forced to watch his team mate from the sidelines, ruefully contemplating whether it had really been worth the effort of swapping teams.

Much play has been made of the simmering aggravation which is alleged to have existed between Peterson and Fittipaldi during 1973, but perhaps too much emphasis has been placed on Emerson's misfortune in late-season races. A bout of wheel trouble certainly did strike at the Lotus team, and whilst it definitely robbed Ronnie of his chances in Brazil, it also put Fittipaldi out of the Dutch Grand Prix later in the season. Late in official practice a front wheel centre pulled out and Emerson's 72 careered into the barrier on a fast swerve just before the Zandvoort pits. He was trapped in the car by his ankles and, although removed with nothing fractured, the reigning World Champion was in such pain and so badly bruised that he was forced to abandon the race after only two laps. And there can be no ground to any suggestion that Chapman acquiesed in encouraging any on-circuit rivalry between the two drivers. In fact the Lotus boss was adamant that Emerson should withdraw from the Dutch Grand Prix if the pain proved insufferable.

There were times during Peterson's year when slight aggravation occasionally mushroomed through that calm Nordic countenance. One such occasion was at Barcelona, on the spectacular, tricky and demanding Montjuich Park road circuit which plunges and races through the city's beautiful public park. Almost one second faster than his closest rival, 'Super-Swede' absolutely dominated the official practice sessions. From the fall of the starter's flag he scorched straight into the lead and evaporated into the distance. Lapping consistently faster than anyone else on the circuit, Ronnie Peterson's move to Team Lotus was about to pay off. Then, unexpectedly, the Lotus broke down.

104

Will he, won't he.........

Extrovert - one of Ronnie's 'party pieces'

"It's his gearbox oil" sniffed Pete Kerr with a knowing look on his face as Ronnie flashed past the pits with 50 laps of the 75 lap race under his belt. Still with March, on this occasion tending the sluggish 731 driven by the undistinguished Henri Pescarolo, Kerr felt rather more concern over 'March's man' out there in front leading the race in a Lotus. And Pete Kerr was right - it was gearbox oil. Ronnie was in trouble. Six laps later Emerson Fittipaldi assumed the lead and a sour faced Peterson walked back to the pits, too angry even to acknowledge the plaudits of the crowd.

Fittipaldi seemed to be living beneath the luck of some benevolent God at this stage of the season. Luck is an integral component of every Grand Prix driver's stock-in-trade, but Emerson seemed to be in receipt of bonus payments at Barcelona. His 72 was slowing drastically, a rear tyre deflating, and it seemed inevitable that he would be caught by Carlos Reutemann's works Brabham. It seemed all over bar the proverbial shouting, but with nine laps to go, Reutemann stopped with a broken driveshaft. Fittipaldi, balancing his car on that almost flat tyre with the delicacy of a seasoned ballet dancer, came home to win his third Grand Prix of the season. The Championship stood with Fittipaldi on 31 points, Stewart on 19. Ronnie Peterson had none.

It looked as though he would win the non-championship Race of Champions, but gearbox trouble intervened. He was leading Stewart in the non-championship International Trophy meeting at Silverstone, only to be caught out by a shower of snow. If there was anything going that was likely to harm his chances, poor old Ronnie seemed to ferret it out. Almost with a purpose.

The Lotus arrangement was a complicated and demanding deal, calling on Chapman's team to provide two cars for each driver. Clearly the World Champion wasn't going to do without a spare and neither was Peterson. After his spell at March, this luxury was new to Ronnie and he certainly appreciated it. But he also used the privilege on one notable occasion. Used it right up to the hilt in fact.

The 1973 Belgian Grand Prix was the subject of more controversy than the rest of that season put together. It was a race hampered by politics, Nationalism and a certain degree of back-biting for it was patently clear that the Flemish circuit of Zolder was not fully prepared for a World Championship event in the state it appeared in prior to 1973. It required the addition of much safety barrier and it required re-surfacing. The organisers bent over backwards to accommodate these demands, but unfortunately the track surface was relaid far too late and the moment Formula 1 cars with their enormous tyres began to practice on it, the top layer of tarmac began to peel away. The surface was transformed into a skating rink, drivers complained that it was impossible attempting to control 450 brakehorsepower on thousands of tiny stones which had the effect of tiny ball bearings on the circuit. The militant members of the Grand Prix Drivers Association reacted to this extremely difficult situation by saying that unless the circuit was in satisfactory trim by race day, they wanted a cast-iron undertaking from the organisers that the race would be cancelled. But the drivers' bill for three and a half million Belgian francs must be paid either way.

The organisers tackled the problem with a purpose. After the first practice day, the new track surface was scraped off by an army of road maintenance machines and, virtually overnight, was relaid with fresh tarmac. Having extracted the agreement of the organisers that the race would be cancelled if the surface was not up to scratch, the drivers cautiously edged their way out to Saturday practice. Yet again it looked as though the race might prove a Peterson benefit, for he took his spare car out and set fastest practice lap of the weekend. The only driver to lap below 1 minute 23 seconds on this 2.62 mile circuit, Peterson started from pole position. But he nearly didn't start at all.

Lotus Competitions Manager Peter Warr is a tall, slim man with a rather scholastic, bespectacled face and an absolute dedication to the job of making Team Lotus the most effective team in Grand Prix racing. At no point during 1973 did Warr, unashamedly a Peterson fan, express even the mildest doubt about the efficiency of the 'joint number one' status which both his drivers enjoyed. He as much as anyone else around the Lotus team could see that SuperSwede was developing into a consistently faster driver than Fittipaldi and although he clearly did everything to ensure that there was no favouritism, there was no doubt that he'd got a soft spot for Ronnie.

But Peter Warr had a very stern disagreement with the Swede on race morning at Zolder. On the Sunday morning of each race, just a few hours before the Grand Prix is scheduled to start, most organisers provide half an hour or an hour of untimed practice. Weary mechanics who spent all the previous night fixing a gearbox or toiling over an engine change can at least have the chance of seeing whether their handiwork has been done properly. Last minute suspension adjustments can be tried, gearboxes can be run in and race day spectators can take a free sample of what's to come later in the afternoon.

Ronnie hadn't been feeling too healthy during the two practice days and by Sunday morning his temperature was running at nearly a hundred degrees. He neither looked particularly healthy nor felt it. But he insisted that he be allowed to take the spare car out for a few more laps of the circuit. "I want more laps to try it" emphasised Ronnie with that rather doleful look of a put-out school boy on his face. But Peter was adamant. There should be no practice.

Eventually it was agreed that Peterson could take his spare 72 out for five laps "and only five laps" to bed in brake pads. So Ronnie swung gently out of the pit lane and drove a couple of gentle laps to check that the brakes were alright before steaming into his fourth lap as fast as possible. After the pits at Zolder the track funnels down into a tight left hander followed by a

His most ardent supporter for the past six years - Barbro

long right hand curve which sweeps the cars through 180 degrees and rushes them up a short straight immediately behind the paddock. Just before the circuit swings left into the country, the organisers installed a tight second gear chicane. As Ronnie Peterson charged up to that chicane on his fourth lap, the moment he touched the brakes, he realised that things were not quite right.

The effort of braking for that tight left hander after the pits had overheated the brakes and glazed those freshly installed pads. "So I tried to go through the corner in the best possible way and hit the fence with the wing. I knocked that off" a contrite Peterson told Peter Warr on his return to the pits. But he was immediately dispatched in his other car and, after a handful of laps, failed to come round again. Eventually the jovial Swede arrived back in the pits seated on the back of Emerson's car. Warr listened in disbelief as Ronnie explained to him that he'd fallen off the road again!

With just a few hours left to go before the Grand Prix started, the pole position man had no car ready to take his place on the starting grid. So while Colin Chapman escorted Peterson off to the medical unit for a quick check up - he'd received a hefty bang on the head as he ploughed down the catch fencing in his second accident - Warr took a deep breath and rallied the Lotus mechanics round to make one good car out of the two bent ones, and make it pretty quickly.

Critics of modern Grand Prix racing oversimplify the case when they scornfully dismiss current 3-litre Formula 1 machines as 'kit cars'. A great deal of specialist components from specialist firms are 'welded' together by highly trained mechanics to complete the assembly of such a car. The word 'kit' implies that the components are universally standardised. But fortunately one Lotus 72 is very much like its stablemate, so although time was short there was little practical difficulty in taking the undamaged rear wing, oil tank and oil cooler off one car and adding it to the rear of the other. As one mechanic was heard to grimly remark "At least he was good enough to crash one forwards and one backwards".

For two laps Ronnie Peterson led the Belgian Grand Prix although by his own admission he shouldn't have been driving that day. Francois Cevert's French-blue Tyrrell hurtled away in the lead as Ronnie gradually faded down into seventh place. "I thought I'd drive for a finish". Ronnie's explanations were getting just the slightest bit repetitive "but some days you just don't want to remember" he explained many months later. His car? Oh yes, the car. Well, that slid off the road on lap 43, careering into the ditch alongside the already-parked McLaren M23 left by Peter Revson. It was the same parking lot already occupied by the Marches of Jean-Pierre Jarier and Mike Beuttler as well as Jackie Oliver's Shadow. It proved to be quite an expensive Formula 1 graveyard!

Ronnie Peterson finally got his Grand Prix score for 1973 off the ground at Monte Carlo where he finished a distant third, lapped by winner

Jackie Stewart and team mate Fittipaldi. By this stage in the season Stewart had already made his decision to retire from driving at the end of the year, a secret which was to remain between him, his entrant Ken Tyrrell and Ford's Walter Hayes until the evening before the United States Grand Prix in October. He was therefore single-minded in his desire to go out with the Championship crown resting firmly on his shoulders and his splendid victory over the reigning title holder in Monaco's sunshine meant that Fittipaldi was down to a four point lead.

Championship prospects motivate some drivers, the thought of winning individual races motivate others. But for a racing car builder, it is the Constructors Championship which provides the objective at which to aim. Colin Chapman's prime purpose in equipping his team with two World class drivers was to secure Lotus, or John Player Special as they were now correctly dubbed, the World Constructors Championship. However, one thing was tacitly understood at the start of the season. Ronnie would do his utmost to help Emerson win the Brazilian Grand Prix and Emerson, in turn, would do his utmost to allow Ronnie to win the Swedish Grand Prix. As things had turned out, Fittipaldi had needed to rely on nobody's assistance at Interlagos and, in any case, he wouldn't have been able to call on Ronnie. But at Anderstorp, venue for the Swedish Grand Prix, the whole affair looked like developing into a demonstration run exactly to plan. And then everything went wrong less than ten laps from the end.

I often wonder just how close business and team colleagues get to Ronnie Peterson. Outwardly he faces the world with a relaxed confidence, his face occasionally creased by either an impish smile or a practised look of blank incredulity. He hides behind what he likes people to think of as a lack of understanding of the English language, but he knows a lot more than he gives away. And despite all the non-commital good honour, by mid-season 1973 it had become painfully obvious that he was consistently quicker than Emerson Fittipaldi. What's more, whilst he took his bad luck early in the season with a quiet sense of resigned disappointment, by the same token he would never compromise any success he enjoyed later in the year by modestly shrugging off any praise. That he was developing into a faster driver than Fittipaldi didn't come as a surprise to him; as far as he was inwardly concerned, he'd always been a faster driver than Emerson. It was just a case of waiting for the opportunity to prove it.

Ronnie knows only one way to drive a racing car and that's flat out! My favourite racing picture hangs over a desk at my home at which I do much of my writing. It shows the start at Anderstorp back in 1973 with Peterson's Lotus laying a jet black trail of rubber from its huge rear tyres as he blasts off the grid to take an immediate lead in front of his home crowd. Behind, team mate Fittipaldi can be seen coming almost diagonally across the track to tuck in behind him and block out both the Tyrrells of Cevert and Stewart. It's terrific stuff, pure team tactics and every time I look at that

111

Ronnie and Barbro with Prince Bertil of Sweden prior to his home Grand Prix at Anderstorp, 1974

picture it seems to epitomise Ronnie's approach. Flat out, all the way.

Peterson set a blistering pace at Anderstorp with Fittipaldi dutifully running second, fending off any challenge from the two Tyrrells. This was the race Ronnie was going to win, no doubt, thought everyone. The crowds cheered him hysterically, the Lotus pit crew grinned fit to bust and everybody in the press room started wondering just *when was* the last time a pair of Colin Chapman's Lotuses had finished a Grand Prix in 1-2 formation. If I'd have been asked, I'd have said at Watkins Glen in 1967. Having written just that later in the year as a magazine caption, I was then deluged with letters from knowledgeable schoolboys telling me I was wrong. The answer, of course, was the 1968 South African Grand Prix, Jimmy Clark's last Formula 1 race.

Jochen Rindt used to have a gremlin which prevented him from finishing motor races, let alone winning them. Time and again between 1966 and 1969 he proved the quickest Grand Prix driver by far, and time and again he lost Grand Prix races. Rindt had been a member of the Lotus team until his sad death in 1970 and one began to wonder whether that gremlin had stayed, unnoticed in the Lotus camp and was latching onto Peterson.

But this time he appeared supremely controlled, going like mad and well in command of the race. But little by little, every one of those runners in the leading bunch encountered slight problems which obliged them to ease their pace. Isolated from the crowds watching his progress, isolated from the men of his team in the pits, when a Grand Prix driver encounters a problem it can be a lonely business sorting it out in the best possible way. He's on his own, for the pressure of achieving race results precludes him from driving into the pits to discuss the difficulty. Years ago, when races were longer and the pressures were less, a driver could make a quick pit stop, perhaps for an adjustment, perhaps for fresh tyres. Nowadays just a single pit stop, just for a very short while, inevitably throws the competitor miles out of contention. It is no overstatement to say that Grand Prix racing in the 1970s is more intensely competitive than at any time in the past. Look at the grid times, look at the margins by which races are won, and then try to argue otherwise.

Behind those pounding Lotus 72s, first it was Cevert who ran into problems. His tyres had picked up some debris from the circuit surface and were now vibrating slightly. Not sufficiently to warrant a visit to the pits, just enough to oblige him to slacken his pace. Stewart slipped ahead into third place and took up his pursuit of the Lotus team. Little by little the Scot closed in on the sleek 72s and Fittipaldi began getting a little bit concerned that he might be forced into making a challenge for the lead owing to the pressure of the Tyrrell. But he managed to stave off the Scot until they were virtually within sight of the chequered flag and, suddenly, he found himself with Denny Hulme on his tail as well. Hulme, the hard-charging craggy New Zealander, could be as fast as anyone else on the track on his day - and he had made up his mind that this was clearly going to be his day.

Fittipaldi was losing his rear brakes, so Peterson's protective shadow fell away, but Ronnie stayed tantalisingly out of reach of the Tyrrell, for Stewart himself found his rear brakes failing as well. But still it looked as though Ronnie might pull it off even though Hulme was closing at a terrific pace. Suddenly it was all over; Hulme went through with just over a lap to go and Ronnie had slowed right down with a puncture. Robbed of that victory which he wished for so dearly, he had to be content with second place. Cevert, by dint of just plugging away, found himself third.

Would Ronnie Peterson *ever* win a Grand Prix?

Happy days ; Smiling with Lotus boss Colin Chapman

Ronnie with Peter Warr, Lotus Competitions Manager. Warr is a complete Peterson fan, extremely impressed with the Swede's total involvement and commitment to driving a racing car flat out all the time

CHAPTER 5
Nice won Ronnie!

EVEN THE DIE-HARD enthusiast cannot fail to concede that John Player and Son, sponsors of the Lotus Grand Prix team, are well on the ball when it comes to advertising their own success. When Emerson Fittipaldi clinched his World Championship at Monza in 1972, their publicity people showered the circuit with stickers proclaiming the new champion's achievement alongside the name of their car. After every Grand Prix won by a John Player Special, there's always somebody ready with a handful of circular stickers announcing the John Player Special as victor in that particular Grand Prix. Rather like the notches on Billy the Kid's revolver, both the Lotuses accumulate these stickers across their rear wings.

By the time those 72s were rolled out of their transporters at the sun-baked Paul Ricard circuit near Marseilles, venue for the 1973 French Grand Prix, their wings were already pretty crowded. In addition to a sticker reminding them that they were Champion Car Constructors, Fittipaldi's wins in Argentina, Brazil and Spain gave an excuse for three more to be added. I'm always tempted to ask what they do with the stickers when the race is won by a Tyrrell, Ferrari, Brabham or McLaren - surely they'll be as much a collector's piece as unperforated Penny Blacks in a few year's time!

But there was still one sticker they hadn't been able to use by that stage in the season. The French Grand Prix was the eighth round of the Championship trail and 'Ronald' as mechanic Keith Leighton referred to him, had still failed to come home with the big result. The pundits were beginning to think that he wouldn't make it, accusations were bandied about that Ronnie couldn't get on terms with the car, he wasn't smooth enough with his driving. One journalist speculated that perhaps the Lotus 72 would teach Peterson a smoother, more relaxed style "like it had done to Rindt". Others simply derided a driver who seemed unable to finish in the results, clearly not even bothering to think at all about the precise reasons behind his retirements. It's little or nothing to do with a driver that a wheel breaks up due to a faulty casting, nor if a gearbox leaks all its oil away.

Perhaps, one or two seasoned observers speculated, he'd do better if he didn't try so hard. Ronnie has always been a fast driver, he freely admits that he doesn't really know any other way to drive a racing car. But the good

115

side of that means that he's the one consistent factor you can rely on when planning a race. His mechanics love him because he's always trying. They're not critical of him if his car breaks, because they know he is working as hard as he knows how. Ronnie Peterson gives his all, every time he sits behind the wheel of a racing car. And that's why many people feel the only advantage a team in the 1970s needs is Mr Peterson sitting in the cockpit of the number one car.

That race at Paul Ricard was memorable in more ways than one. McLaren Racing chose it as their opportunity to debut Jody Scheckter in one of the team's M23s and this unassuming 23 year old South African proved the sensation of practice. He started from the front row of the grid between Stewart's pole winning Tyrrell and Fittipaldi's Lotus and led straight off the line, staying ahead of the regular aces for no fewer than 43 of the race's 54 laps. Peterson sustained problems with his car's fuel system during practice which meant that he had to start the race from the second row of the grid. That didn't matter; he made a fine start and joined in the leading bunch trying to out-flank Scheckter's fast McLaren. In fact he led the attack for the first few laps, but eventually just couldn't work out what to do about it and waved Fittipaldi past to see if he could do any better.

What happened in that race seems to have been a source of much controversy ever since. Certainly Peterson didn't show any of those earlier indications of impetuosity. He waited and watched behind his team mate who clearly wasn't going to have a better chance of passing the well driven McLaren. Running with a flatter rear wing than his rivals, Jody was able to out-run them down the long straights, and whilst he could stay ahead by dint of holding his rivals up through the twisty section, there seemed to be no legitimate way he could be passed.

With nine laps to go, Emerson decided to employ one of his favourite harassment techniques. Rushing up close behind Jody on a tight right hander, Emerson slipped the black chisel nose of his Lotus up the inside of the McLaren, intent on intimidating Scheckter into letting him past. But that didn't impress Jody one little bit. He stuck resolutely to his line and tried to take the corner. The M23's right rear tyre ran over Fittipaldi's left front wheel and suddenly Scheckter was airborne. Fittipaldi slithered to a halt with the front suspension of his Lotus smashed and crushed while Jody attempted to give chase but quickly found himself obliged to stop with his McLaren in a rather second-hand state.

Back in the pits the recriminations began. Fittipaldi's South American temperament exploded in front of the McLaren pits. He asked Jody what the hell he thought he was doing. Scheckter replied that he didn't really care whether he was World Champion or not ... the accident had been Emerson's fault. Denny Hulme remarked philosophically after the race "I was trying to get up there to tell you, kid! That Fittipaldi always pulls those tricks".

But out on the circuit, suddenly everyone realised that Ronnie was in the lead, well ahead of Francois Cevert's Tyrrell. Nine laps later, with Colin Chapman ecstatically performing his victory leap on the track by the finishing line, Ronnie won his very first Grand Prix motor race at his fortieth attempt. The Moet et Chandon bubbled over, a beaming Peterson donned a huge victory garland and a little man appeared from nowhere to slap another of those John Player stickers onto the front of his overalls. It read "1st, Nice won Ronnie!"

Barbro timing Ronnie's progress in the 1974 French Grand Prix, his second win of the year

RONNIE PETERSON

Results speak for themselves and while Ronnie doesn't try to conceal his pleasure at his own achievement, one couldn't accuse him of exactly shouting about them. For his victory parade lap he was bundled into an open car and sent off with second man Cevert and third man Carlos Reutemann. The handsome Francois, idolised by thousands of car-crazy Frenchmen, was almost as delighted as Ronnie, for he'd at least taken second place in front of his many admirers. He monopolised the attention as they cruised round the victory lap, sitting high on the back of the car, a born extrovert. In fact Ronnie was so unruffled that Mike Hailwood, waiting at the back of the circuit with his recalcitrant Surtees TS14, didn't quite appreciate it was Ronnie who'd won the race.

"They came round" laughed Mike "with old Francois waving to the crowd as if he'd won the bloody race, almost keeping a right hand on Ronnie's shoulder to keep him down in the seat. I thought, well that's funny, I'd have thought Mad Ronald won that one but it was obviously the Good Francois. Bloody funny, that". But he was right, 'Mad Ronald', as 'Mike the Bike' always used to call him jokingly to his face, had won a Grand Prix at last.

To those involved on a full-time basis with Grand Prix racing, there is a hectic fortnightly schedule to be adhered to from the end of April until the beginning of October. Every other weekend in the summer, there is some round of the World Championship taking place somewhere. And in 1973 it was the turn of Silverstone, the acknowledged traditional home of British motor racing since the Second World War, to host the British Grand Prix.

Somehow, despite its obvious ancestry as an old airfield, Silverstone manages to exude an air of gentility. It's not exactly Ascot, but it's about as near to it as you're going to get in Grand Prix racing. Whereas Monaco is definitely the place for the extrovert rich, just as Brands Hatch caters for the hot dog and hamburger brigade, Silverstone contrives to remain slightly aloof. It combines the atmosphere of a garden party with the spectacle of Grand Prix racing at its best.

If you visit Silverstone in the middle of winter, you can't imagine in your wildest dreams how on earth it could be the sight of some spectacular sport like motor racing. Basically it's flat and uninspiring. But in fact it's the fastest road course in Britain, where Grand Prix cars seldom drop below 110 mph anywhere on its 2.7 mile lap. For those who reckon the art of high speed cornering died when Grand Prix cars developed their huge rear tyres, well, they haven't seen a Grand Prix at Silverstone. And 1973 provided some Grand Prix.

Elated by his French Grand Prix triumph, Ronnie started the ninth round of the Championship from pole position flanked by the McLarens of Hulme and Peter Revson. Colin Chapman was delighted, for he'd had his hands more than full during practice administering the team's affairs as Peter Warr had been forced to take some time off owing to trouble with a slipped disc. The only place to watch at Silverstone is Woodcote, a 150 mph fifth gear right hander which cails for ability, a perfect car and nerves of steel to take absolutely flat out. Or as near flat out as is possible. Needless to say, Peterson got closer than anyone else!

Having been jumped by Stewart on the opening lap, Peterson got a second chance at Silverstone. Jody Scheckter obliged him by causing what looked like the World's biggest accident when he ran wide at Woodcote at the end of the opening lap. As Jody's M23 spun backwards across the circuit in front of the rest of the field, cars scattered and collided like a bunch of frightened rabbits. When the dust cleared, about one third of the entire field had been damaged in some way or another and the organisers took the decision to stop the race. It was restarted over an hour later after Andrea de Adamich had been cut from the wreckage of his works Brabham BT42 and taken off to hospital.

Ronnie was complaining that his Lotus oversteered a shade too much, but despite this slight impediment, threw himself into the second race with a vengeance. Fighting to stave off Stewart's Tyrrell, the sight of Peterson hurling his car at Woodcote and negotiating the corner with howls of protest flying from his rear tyres and his arms working away at the wheel as though he were conducting the London Philharmonic, sent a surge of excitement through even the most blase spectator.

Later in the race, Stewart tried to pass Ronnie in much the same way Fittipaldi had tried to pass Scheckter at Ricard, but the Lotus lad wasn't having any of that and closed the door at Stowe corner so violently that the next thing JYS knew was he was in the middle of a cornfield! That was one race that Ronnie seemed certain to win on sheer guts and ability, but it wasn't to be. He eventually took second place behind Revson's McLaren, inches ahead of Hulme's similar car and James Hunt's Hesketh March 731. The trouble? "Oh, it was oversteering much too much" remarked Ronnie casually. As Pete Lyons remarked in *Autosport*; "If Ronnie Peterson complained of too much oversteer, then it must have been bad!" Quite so.

The next few Grand Prix events came and went, Fittipaldi falling increasingly into Stewart's clutches and Peterson losing both the Dutch and German races with mechanical problems. Then came the two races at Osterreichring and Monza, races which virtually decided that Emerson Fittipaldi would leave the Lotus team.

"Anything I can do to help Emerson win the Championship, I'll do". A sweat stained Ronnie climbed into the Goodyear bus in the Osterreichring paddock, happy to be away from the bright sunshine and the crowds of happy autograph hunters who seemed intent on snaring him. Fittipaldi was already there waiting. Without any prompting, Emerson moved forward to his team mate and clutched his arm. The Brazilian didn't have to say anything, it was obvious from his eyes, flushed with emotion, that he wished to express his genuine gratitude. "Any time" grinned Ronnie sheepishly as he settled into a seat alongside Barbro and began swigging a Coca Cola. Ronnie had just won the Austrian Grand Prix after Fittipaldi's leading Lotus dropped out with a disconnected line in its fuel system. There had been only six laps left to run and Peterson dutifully stayed behind Fittipaldi having actually waved him through into the lead on lap 18. Even though he'd been cruelly robbed of victory, Emerson could have no doubts whatsoever as to the calibre of the man he had been teamed with.

The Italian Grand Prix at Monza looked like being the scene of Fittipaldi's final last-ditch stand in an effort to retain his Championship. Emerson's fortunes, hampered ever since his Zandvoort shunt by painful ankles, would have to take a dramatic swing upwards to enable him to go to the final North American races with more than a remote mathematical possibility of being Champion again. By contrast, Stewart looked a virtual certainty for the title, holding a confident 19 points lead over his rival as the Monza race got underway.

Victory ; Sharing the victory rostrum at Osterreichring with Jackie Stewart (left) and Carlos Pace after winning the 1973 Austrian Grand Prix, a race which he initially handed to Fittipaldi and then won after Emerson's car broke down in the race's closing stages

But Fittipaldi was nursing a secret by this stage, something about which he'd not yet told Chapman but a secret on which the press were just beginning to elbow in. Emerson now lived in Switzerland with his wife, brother and parents and as such was ideally placed for discussions with the Philip Morris tobacco concern, an organisation getting increasingly impatient for their two year deal with the BRM team to expire. They wanted Fittipaldi to be one of their contracted drivers for 1974 and McLaren boss Teddy Mayer fancied some of that Marlboro sponsorship for his cars. In addition, it seemed more than likely that Texaco would go wherever Fittipaldi went, so the prospect of welding Marlboro and Texaco together as co-sponsors of the McLaren team, with Fittipaldi as number one, looked most inviting. At the same time, Brabham boss Bernie Ecclestone was wooing Emerson with a similar proposition, but this wasn't quite so attractive to the canny Brazilian for Bernie preferred on keeping Carlos Reutemann as the second driver.

Discussions were well advanced by the time the Championship trail arrived at Monza and the race proved to be a high speed procession with Peterson and Fittipaldi, running in nose to tail formation, leading the field. Ronnie was in front, where he rightly belonged on the strength of pole position and a searing getaway when the starter's flag dropped. The only fair and legitimate way for Emerson to win the race would have been to jump the start from his place on row two and get away first from the word go. But once the die had been cast, once those two 72s had appeared at the end of their first lap with Ronnie in front, it would have been absurd team tactics to allow Emerson to risk the race by dicing with his team mate. No, the order had to come from Colin Chapman - he was the man who had to make the decision. Was it reasonable for Ronnie Peterson to concede the Italian Grand Prix in a vain effort to sustain Fittipaldi's title hopes?

Quite clearly it wasn't a reasonable burden for Peterson to shoulder. By now obviously a consistently faster driver, just how many other events would Ronnie be obliged to hand over to Emerson if this course of action was followed? So whilst Fittipaldi sat behind, waiting, Chapman decided to do nothing about it until he saw where Stewart would finish. However, Ronnie was fully aware of what was going on.

"I would have gladly let Emerson through if Jackie had finished fifth" Ronnie insists with a generosity he no longer had to prove "but I was going to leave it as long as possible. I was being shown the boards and when Jackie moved into fourth place, I reckoned that was it". The two black and gold Lotuses swept out of Parabolica, along in front of the pits and across the line with Peterson taking his third Grand Prix win of the year. And one which was quite justifiable.

The sports page of a Milan newspaper next day carried an article, allegedly by Fittipaldi, saying how dismayed he was at "Colin Chapman's failure to keep my Championship chances open". This was fighting stuff from the deposed Champion and seemed a virtual confirmation that he

Controversial win. Ronnie leads Emerson at Monza during the 1973 Italian Grand Prix, a race which many people feel Ronnie should have given to Emerson to keep the Brazilian's Championship chances open a little longer. But how many more races would Ronnie have been obliged to concede?

Elation. Ronnie holds his trophy high over his head after winning the 1974 Monaco Grand Prix in the 'old' Lotus 72. Princess Grace, Prince Rainier and Barbro share the occasion

would be leaving Lotus after the Watkins Glen race. Ronnie seemed a bit disappointed in Emerson's rather hostile reaction, and I spent all the following Monday evening trying to track down the Brazilian driver to his Swiss lair. Finally I got through to him late that evening and asked him about the stories in the Italian papers.

"They say you feel Ronnie shouldn't have been allowed to win" I started. There was a brief silence and I could almost see Emerson's mischievious grin coming down the receiver. "Oh" he said casually, "You know those Italian papers, they're always exaggerating". I realised I'd got the message - he was disappointed alright!

"I'm not sure when Emerson signed for Marlboro McLaren" reflects Ronnie in his more thoughtful moments, "but I don't think he was fully concentrating by the time we got to the end of the year". That might be rather an injustice, but one suspects that Peterson's instant brilliance with the Lotus 72 led Fittipaldi to suspect that the Swede was getting better machinery. Peter Warr utterly refutes this suggestion, and quite rightly too. For Ronnie's confidence and ability to come to terms with just about any circuit around tends to disarm his rivals' confidence, almost before practice has got underway.

An incident at Mosport Park, the Canadian Grand Prix circuit near Toronto, highlighted this disarming air of casual confidence which Peterson can turn on, knowing full well that he will back it up by an on-track performance if he's called on to do so. Warr was offered a set of special Goodyear intermediates for use in the race, Goodyear's racing staff automatically assuming that Ronnie would be the rightful recipient. Even though Emerson was by now settled on leaving Lotus, Peter explained at some length to the bemused technicians that he'd got two top drivers contracted and that meant that they must have equal equipment. But there was only one set available and that was that.

Peterson heard about this apparent 'problem' almost by accident. He grinned, turned to Warr and told him to fit the tyres to Emerson's car - "I'll win on what you give me". Peter Warr has dealt with many drivers in his time, but this attitude simply left him flabbergasted. Unfortunately Ronnie didn't win the race, ironically sliding into a barrier and damaging the rear suspension while he was running right in front of Emerson. It proved to be a chaotic race thrown into disorder by a spate of pit stops to change cars onto dry weather tyres after the soaking surface dried out 20 laps into the race. Much of the race was confused owing to the organisers losing control of their official lap chart and, after many hours of post-race argument which lasted well into the evening, Peter Revson was posted as the winner in his Yardley McLaren. Fittipaldi was second, although many independent lap charters think to this day he was the rightful victor, and Jack Oliver's Shadow was third. The man who was really browned off by the whole business was Jean-Pierre Beltoise, the dour little Frenchman who was driving a BRM.

Two laps from the end, he let Oliver and Fittipaldi go past him without realising they were on the same lap. Beltoise reckoned he was in second place and he was right. But he just waved the third and fourth place men past, demoting himself two places in one unknowing manoeuvre. It was that sort of race!

Traditionally Watkins Glen, the picturesque road circuit in Northern New York States, hosts the final round of the World Championship. The United States Grand Prix has traditionally been a 'big money' finale to the championship trail with a 50,000 dollar first prize acting as a carrot to the attendant 180 mph rabbits. The 1973 race provided the usual frantic practice efforts, much of the action on the track backed up by intense speculation as to where various drivers would be moving to in 1974. One of the most vehemently denied rumours was that of Fittipaldi to McLaren. Thus, with that age old peversity and blood hound obstinacy which every journalist seems to nurture in some quantity, that old story was certain to be true.

But Watkins Glen was a sad finale to a fine year. The beaming Francois Cevert, on the verge of assuming the role of Tyrrell team leader from a retiring Jackie Stewart, never came back from Saturday morning practice. His blue Tyrrell cannoned off the circuit into the guard rail in the near flat-out Esses to be ripped asunder by an impact that the handsome Frenchman could not survive. A cloud of misery hovered over everybody in the pits and not even Ronnie Peterson's brilliant pole position could hide the depression in the Lotus camp at the end of the day. On the lap before he died, Francois had established second fastest time and would almost certainly have started the United States Grand Prix from the place alongside Ronnie on the front row of the grid.

But 24 hours later the skies looked brighter again and Team Lotus was 50,000 dollars better off. Ronnie had led the United States Grand Prix from start to finish, staving off a challenge from James Hunt's Hesketh March 731 which seemed to harry him all the way. Immediately SuperSwede was swept away amidst a sea of excited supporters while Fittipaldi quietly finished sixth. It was his last drive for Team Lotus. Three months later he would face Ronnie as his closest competitor from the seat of a bright red and white Marlboro-Texaco McLaren M23.

John Player Team Lotus were World Champion Car Constructors. The team system with two drivers both capable of winning races had been completely vindicated. Although Fittipaldi's hopes of retaining his Championship had been dashed, for Peterson the situation was different. With Stewart's retirement, the way into 1974 looked extremely bright and promising. His career, it seemed, could only go upwards to the Championship. Already Lotus had given him the tools necessary to win four Grand Prix races, so 1973 had been more than memorable in itself.

Personal ambition is the over-riding motivation of any Grand Prix   **125** racing driver. Races and Championships are what matters and Peterson in leaving March, and Fittipaldi in leaving Lotus, took what they thought were the only correct steps in pursuit of fulfilment of these ambitions. When Peterson handed Fittipaldi the lead of the 1973 Austrian Grand Prix, he made a supremely generous gesture to keep his team mate's Championship hopes open.

But generous gestures do not win motor races. It is rare for a fellow competitor to receive such assistance from a colleague in Grand Prix races today, such is the pressure of competition. Perhaps by doing so, Ronnie Peterson emphasised to the world his confidence in his own ability. A confidence so great that he could afford to be generous.

Ronnie in action during that post-British GP cricket match

CHAPTER 6
A Championship lost

"CAN YOU IMAGINE - Ronnie stood for an hour in the garage alongside Ickx before he realised that he wasn't running number two!" Peter Warr must have felt pretty confident as he teased his number one in the scorching paddock at Buenos Aires just before practice began for the 1974 Argentine Grand Prix. Ronnie, who'd run as number two to Fittipaldi's number one throughout 1973, had forgotten that his car carried number one for the start of 1974. Usually this privilege is reserved for the World Champion driver of the previous year but, with Stewart retired, in 1974 it was carried by the number one car in the team that won the Constructors' Championship. And in 1974 that car was driven by Ronnie Peterson.

Those two opening Grand Prix races of the season, in Argentina and Brazil, provide a welcome respite from a European winter. Most drivers and teams stay out for the fortnight between the two events and try to squeeze in a holiday. From that point on, the Championship calendar closes in around them and there's little chance of snatching more than a few days off until after the United States Grand Prix in October.

Only three months had passed since Ronnie's brilliant flag to flag victory at Watkins Glen, so Lotus were still relying on the faithful old Lotus 72. The new 76 - or the JPS/9 as Lotus' major sponsor John Player wanted the car titled - would not be ready until the South African Grand Prix owing to slow progress back at the factory forced on by the energy crisis in Britain and the resultant three day week. With Emerson Fittipaldi facing the world from the cockpit of a gaudy red and white McLaren M23, Ronnie's team mate was now Belgian driver Jacky Ickx, back at the wheel of a Cosworth powered car for the first time since he drove for Jack Brabham in 1969. Ickx had been a Ferrari team member since the start of the 1970 season but had never managed to string together more than a few brief winning streaks. Clearly one of the world's fastest drivers when the Ferrari flat-12 would allow him to be, Ickx had suffered intolerable pressure from the Italian press who seemed determined to heap all the blame for Ferrari's indifferent years in 1972 and 1973 onto his shoulders. Now the courteous Belgian had quit; he'd had enough. Colin Chapman had been unable to secure Jody Scheckter's services alongside Ronnie for 1974, so the logical choice amongst those who remained was Ickx. He signed a two year contract to drive for Chapman's team.

Ironically, the great surprise of the 1974 Argentine Grand Prix, indeed the great surprise of the 1974 season, was the return of Ferrari's form. Not since Ickx's 1970 season would the Prancing Horse come so close to winning the World Championship. With Clay Regazzoni and Niki Lauda driving, Ferrari threw down the gauntlet in the practice sessions round the colourful Parque Almirante Brown in Buenos Aires. For a time it looked as though Regazzoni's 1 minute 50.96 second lap would be fast enough for pole position. But Ronnie went out, picked up the gauntlet and threw it straight back into Ferrari's face with a terrific 1 minute 50.78 second lap virtually as the chequered flag came out to mark the end of practice. He had started 1974 as he'd finished 1973; on top.

"We've had nearly six hours of practice and what I haven't learned over the past couple of days, I'm not about to find out in half an hour this morning". Ronnie lay in the sun by the swimming pool at Buenos Aires' swish Sheraton Hotel early on race morning, Barbro watching over him with a grin as she finished sewing some fresh John Player Special patches onto his new overalls. Lotus was one of the few teams not to avail themselves of untimed practice that morning even though team manager Peter Warr made his way out to the circuit at an early hour. His drivers might not have been there, but Warr's stopwatch carefully plotted the performance of Lotus' rivals. Nobody improved significantly. Ronnie, back at the pool, described to me in great detail an accident which he'd had at the wheel of a 2-litre Lola sports car in Buenos Aires back in 1971. The car had somehow managed to execute a backward roll at around 150 mph, somersaulted in mid-air and then come crashing down onto its tail and then bounced back onto its four punctured tyres. "I knew bloody flying was never for me" he grinned. "Still, we did win the next year's race in the Ferrari. That was a better way to start the season!"

For the first ten laps of the Argentine Grand Prix, Ronnie fought to stay with Carlos Reutemann's Brabham BT44 after his front row partner Regazzoni had precipitated a major shunt on the first corner. Both the UOP Shadows of Peter Revson and Jean-Pierre Jarier piled into each other as a result and were instantly out of the contest. Eventually Ronnie slipped back to fourth, then to seventh and finally came into the pits on lap 41 where a deflated rear tyre was changed and a fresh battery fitted. He eventually finished unlucky 13th, five laps down on winner Denis Hulme's McLaren M23. Ickx's sister car stopped on lap 36 with transmission trouble.

Ronnie sat in the Lotus garage staring blankly at the car for some time after the race was over. Barbro methodically packed all his spare racing gear into a soft holdall. I was rushing round the paddock trying to find out just what had happened to everyone prior to jumping on board an airliner for the gruelling 17 hour 'race' back to London. "Where are you going

128

before Brazil?'' I enquired. Barbro shrugged her shoulders. ''I want to go to Lima'' she replied ''but Ronnie wants to go to Interlagos''. I smiled to myself and made a mental bet that they'd end up at Interlagos. They did!

Two weeks later things didn't look much better. For the Brazilian Grand Prix, Ronnie qualified his 72 fourth fastest behind Fittipaldi, Reutemann and Niki Lauda's Ferrari. Colin Chapman had brought out fresh suspension components for the car which made an improvement to the car's handling and Ronnie made an effort to combat the high G-forces generated at Interlagos by attaching strands of string to the side of his helmet, one going down to the shoulder of his overalls and one across to the side of the cockpit. Everyone thought at the time he wasn't feeling very well, but that wasn't really so.

Action in the Lotus pits as mechanics rush to change all four wheels on Ronnie's Lotus 72 during a practice stop, Anderstorp 1974

RONNIE PETERSON

After three laps, Ronnie took the lead from Reutemann and this time held on in front for 15 laps. Then Fittipaldi went through to the front and Ronnie began to realise that his car wasn't handling properly. The cause was a deflating rear tyre again, so on lap 19 he came in for a change and then spent the rest of the race climbing back up to his eventually finishing position, sixth. After the race Ronnie felt very weak indeed, drank too much cold water too quickly and then fell victim to some painful cramp in his chest and suffered some difficulty drawing his breath. A glucose injection helped matters and, after a day's rest he was able to fly home to Europe on the Monday evening.

Before the Grand Prix teams reassembled again at Kyalami at the end of March, Lotus took the opportunity to unveil their brand new Formula 1 car. The venue chosen for the announcement of the Ralph Bellamy designed car was the fashionable New London Theatre where the hundreds of guests were entertained to an excellently balanced, but nonetheless staged, interview between well known television personality William Franklin and Colin Chapman. Franklin asked all the pertinent questions about how the new car - dubbed incidentally JPS/9 for the benefit of John Player and Sons - had been evolved. To even the hardened and sceptical, Lotus appeared to have done it all again. Lightened, more refined and slimmer than the Lotus 72 which it was intended to supersede, the JPS/9 sported such striking novelties as a biplane rear wing and an electrically operated clutch enabling two pedal control. It looked a logical and sensible development along proven lines. Everyone present applauded the whole concept and the reception was rounded off by a promotional film made the previous year entitled "If you're not winning, you're not trying". Oh how wrong that title was! Throughout the rest of 1974 Lotus didn't do a great deal of winning. But they certainly *did* a great deal of trying.

Preparations for the South African Grand Prix meant that there could only be a single car spared for the Race of Champions at Brands Hatch in early March and, similarly, there would only be one entry for the International Trophy meeting at Silverstone a couple of weeks after the Kyalami race. With the two new Lotuses being prepared for South Africa, Ickx drove a 72 at Brands Hatch where he won a fine victory in the streaming rain, leaving Peterson the Silverstone date and the new car.

But first came Kyalami. Everyone uses Kyalami as an excuse for grabbing two or three extra days away from the dismal European winter. The entire racing set takes over the elegant Kyalami Ranch motel less than a mile from the circuit. There's plenty of time for swimming, sunbathing, tennis. It's even possible to slip in some motor racing!

Kyalami has a predominantly 'holiday' atmosphere surrounding it as far as the European teams are concerned, at least that's the way it usually is. But the 1974 South African Grand Prix took place beneath a shroud of unhappiness and with the UOP Shadow team conspicuously absent from the

With Jacky Ickx trying the cockpit of Lotus' new 76, Peterson and Chapman squat beside the new Ralph Bellamy designed car at its unveiling in London, February 1974

starting grid. Just over a week before the race, Peter Revson died in a violent testing accident at the wheel of his new Shadow DN3. Despite medical attention being rushed to his aid, the enormous impact sustained when the Californian's car crashed at virtually undiminished speed into an armco barrier left him with no chance of survival. It was an accident which again revealed the smouldering discontent over the siting of such guard rails at racing circuits, barriers which had been erected with the cause of safety in mind but which were now proving to be killers time and again.

As far as Lotus were concerned, the race turned out to be an unmitigated disaster. Neither car performed well in practice owing to a variety of suspension, tyre and clutch problems and Ronnie was actually slower than Jacky when the times were finally issued. Going into the first corner, Ronnie found his throttle sticking open as he lifted his foot. Before he could hit the ignition switch, he'd punted Ickx up the gearbox and both Lotuses slid off into the catch fence entwined together. They completed just a few more laps each before stopping. Colin Chapman was strapped securely into a London-bound South African Airways Boeing 747 almost before the race had finished. The next day a local newspaper carried an enormous colour picture, taken from a police helicopter, of the two Lotus 76s sitting nose-to-nose in the catch fence at Crowthorne Corner. "I don't think that's very funny" said Ronnie when he saw it. Then he burst out laughing.

It's a measure of a driver's true calibre as to just how he behaves when things are going wrong. There are several Grand Prix drivers currently racing who can turn in brilliant performances when the right set of circumstances prevail in their favour. But to pull back from the brink of disaster and utter demoralisation when everything seems to be going wrong all round you requires a special brand of tenacity. That characteristic is present in Ronnie Peterson's heart and proved his one trait which was tested time and again throughout 1974. Having entered the year on the crest of a wave of success, he now had to suffer ignominy and disillusionment.

The new Lotus was clearly not proving a success from the word go. Despite leading the International Trophy for many laps, Ronnie eventually ground to a standstill with engine failure and walked back to the pits just in time to see James Hunt take the winner's laurels for the very first time in Formula 1. As the crowds cheered Hunt, who won his victory at the wheel of Lord Hesketh's locally built car, Peterson was left to reflect that he had but a single point in the World Championship with three races completed. And the way things were going, his prospects hardly looked as though they were going to improve.

Once the European season gets going, there is a World Championship Grand Prix taking place every fortnight. Preparation, transportation and organisation of one's existing Grand Prix cars leaves precious little time to sort out new machinery. And the expense of maintaining a separate research and development department is sufficiently crippling to ensure that at least

Pensive. Chapman and Peterson study a problem with the new Lotus 76

one Formula 1 team never carried out any testing whatsoever in 1974 outside official timed sessions at the Grand Prix races. Thus, by the time the teams arrived at Madrid's sinuous Jarama circuit to practice for the Spanish Grand Prix at the end of April, six months of non-stop work stretched out in front of them.

In an effort to rustle both JPS/9 and JPS/10 (Ickx's new car) into a state of competitiveness, Lotus had been hard at work. The electric clutch system had been abandoned; it was simply something else to go wrong at a time when the car's fundamental track performance posed the principal problem. Originally designed for tiny 10 inch front and twelve inch rear

133

Leading the 1974 Spanish GP at Jarama in the Lotus 76 from the Ferraris of Niki Lauda and Clay Regazzoni, Jacky Ickx's Lotus 76 and Emerson Fittipaldi's McLaren M23

tyres, the new Lotus suffered extensive suspension changes in an effort to make it behave on larger tyres after Goodyear decreed the 'twelves' and 'tens' to be purely experimental. The double decker rear wing was abandoned and a different oil tank fitted at the rear. Ronnie was still optimistic.

In fact, things looked good for the two Lotus entries as the field lined up in the sheeting rain at the start of the Spanish Grand Prix. Peterson had qualified second quickest alongside Lauda's Ferrari and Ickx sat on the inside of the third row, fifth fastest. For 20 of the race's 80 laps, Ronnie led Niki in the streaming rain with Ickx lying a steady fourth behind Regazzoni. Then it all went wrong. The track began to dry out as the rain stopped and suddenly the deeply grooved, soft compound rain tyres were no longer suitable. It would be necessary for just about everyone to stop and change onto slick racing covers. In one big rush, everyone made for the pits between laps 20 and 25, and the ensuing result was a degree of chaos one wouldn't expect from an Ealing Studios comedy. Towering head and shoulders above their rivals was the Ferrari team whose sportscar racing expertise showed up everybody around them. Whilst Lotus struggled to change wheels, inadvertently letting Ickx drive off down the pit lane with a wheel brace still attached and then having his car's automatic fire extinguisher discharge, Ferrari dispatched each of their cars in less than half a minute. The net result was that Lauda and Regazzoni cruised brilliantly from that point on to a crushing 1-2 victory, no other car even remaining on the same lap by the finish. As for Ronnie "the bloody thing blew up again" was his sole observation as he climbed, grim-faced, from JPS/9.

Once Ronnie had fallen from the Belgian Grand Prix with a leaking fuel bag and Ickx retired with an overheating engine, Colin Chapman took stock of the situation afresh. Not only were JPS/9 and JPS/10 failing to work, the process of making them fully raceworthy was something which he now realised wasn't going to be achieved without three or four week's consistent attention. "But there's no time" explained Peter Warr ruefully "so Colin decided to take a very bold step and shelve them for the time being".

Bold the decision certainly was. Risky it certainly was. But it was also exactly right and extremely well timed. Colin Chapman brought back his brace of Lotus 72s for the Monaco Grand Prix at the end of May. In turn, Ronnie repaid his boss' audacious move by winning the most memorable race of his career. Appropriately enough this win was to come in the same sunlit streets round which he'd won his Formula 3 spurs and first scored Championship points in a Grand Prix car.

Practice turned out to be a ferocious tussle between the two Ferraris which monopolised the front row of the grid with Lauda four tenths of a second quicker than his team mate. But third fastest was Ronnie, the only other driver on the grid to join the front row men in that exclusive sub - 1 minute 27.7 second bracket. Both Peter Warr and Colin Chapman felt more optimistic about their team's prospects than they'd done for a long

135

while as they waited in the Mediterranean sunshine for the start of the Grand Prix.

One last minute disappointment lay in store for the French driver Patrick Depailler. After a brilliant practice effort in his new Tyrrell, his hard-earned fourth place on the grid melted away on the warming up lap when he discovered that one of his car's fuel tanks was leaking. Hurriedly he was strapped into the spare car in the pit lane but didn't have time to rejoin the grid. Down went the starter's flag, Regazzoni's rear wheels spun furiously on the hot tarmac and the Swiss' Ferrari boiled off into the first right hand corner inches in front of his team mate. Depailler's absence allowed Jean-Pierre Jarier's Shadow to move right up alongside Peterson on the inside as they all jostled for the first corner, so Ronnie had to concede the line to the Frenchman. Up the long hill into Casino Square they filed, ear-splitting exhaust notes bouncing off the high walls with Regazzoni, Lauda, Jarier and Peterson in front. They were the lucky ones.

About one third the way down the field, Hulme's McLaren and Beltoise's BRM locked wheels and cannoned off each other into the guard rails which line the circuit. Fittipaldi, well down the pack and suffering from a nasty touch of flu, just squeezed his McLaren through without any drama a split second before his two colleagues were collected by Merzario's Iso-Marlboro, Pace's Surtees, Brambilla's March, Redman's Shadow and Schenken's Trojan. Amidst a flurry of fibreglass, a screeching of tyres and a clanging of metal barriers all these cars were out of the Grand Prix there and then. Nobody was hurt and all the drivers tried to laugh it off nervously.

Ronnie completed the opening lap hard on Jarier's heels and then moved into second place on lap three. Hardly had he done so than he then made an untypical error at the very tight Rascasse hairpin which swings the cars back up past the pits, spinning the Lotus within the tight confines of the narrow circuit. Scheckter swerved his Tyrrell to the outside and just managed to scrape by between the errant Lotus and the firm guard rail. Reutemann was not so lucky. His white Brabham was launched over Ronnie's front wheel, crashing down with deranged suspension. As the Argentinian trailed into his pit and retired from the race, Ronnie sped through, indicating to his pit that he had spun.

It is rare for a driver to be able to pull back such a handicap that Ronnie seemed to face. For ten laps he chased Hailwood's Yardley McLaren, inheriting fifth place when Mike the Bike crashed into the wall very heavily at the Massenet corner just before Casino Square. That gave Ronnie just the taste he needed. Hurling the 72 round the streets with a brilliant brand of controlled abandon, one's mind was cast back four years to the time that Jochen Rindt produced a miracle with the outdated Lotus 49. Now, in 1974, the 72 was as outdated as the 49 had been in 1970. But another great driver's magic looked like reaping for Chapman a similar reward.

On lap 18 Scheckter was passed by the flying black and gold Lotus.

Two laps later Regazzoni spun away his lead at Rascasse and this promoted Ronnie to third. Jarier fought for all he was worth, but his resistance was really rather puny by comparison with Ronnie's ability and, after Pescarolo had baulked the Shadow badly at St Devote, Ronnie moved up into second place as they rushed up towards Casino Square. But there was still Lauda in front, the Austrian confidently leading the race in that apparently invincible flat-12 Ferrari.

"Whew, that Peterson ..." growled a thoughtful Denny Hulme, soaking up the sun from a wall halfway up to Casino Square, "he's certainly going some". That must have been the understatement of the weekend. He was edging ever so slightly closer to Lauda's Ferrari every lap until suddenly Niki's engine started to sound extremely rough. The same overheated ignition problems which caused Niki's retirement at Kyalami had cropped up again. And from lap 33 Ronnie Peterson was leading the race in brilliant style.

He never let up for an instant and he never made a mistake over the remaining 45 laps. Shattering Emerson Fittipaldi's 1973 record, SuperSwede powered his way over the finishing line to score his first Grand Prix victory of 1974. Chapman, ecstatic at this sudden upswing in Lotus fortunes, embraced his man. And the man from John Player at last had an excuse to plant one of those stickers on Ronnie's overalls for the very first time that season!

Things were changing at Lotus during 1974. For one thing, Chapman allowed his two drivers to compete in other categories of racing with different teams. Hitherto the Lotus boss had always protected his investment by insisting that his drivers' contracts with Lotus should be exclusive. But in 1974 Jacky Ickx drove for the works Matra team and the works Alfa-Romeo team on occasions while Ronnie had a saloon contract with BMW and actually enjoyed a one-off drive in a Formula 2 March-BMW at Karlskoga. Lotus were not competing in Formula 2 during 1974, the unreliable and uncompetitive Texaco Star project having been shelved.

At least that Karlskoga drive provided him with some consolation after the Swedish Grand Prix. After only eight laps Ronnie was out of his home Grand Prix with a broken half shaft on the Lotus 72, his only glint of solace coming from the fact that he'd been the only other car to live with the two Tyrrells on this occasion. Less than a fortnight later he had a close escape with the 72 when a brake pad broke up at Zandvoort and he crashed off the end of the main straight. One of the wooden poles supporting the safety catch fencing caught him a glancing blow on the side of his helmet, knocking him unconscious. He was whipped away to the local hospital where he came round after a couple of hours. This stage of the season wasn't an appropriate time to ask Ronnie how he thought things were going!

The summer months rolled by with a variety of fortunes for the disillusioned Lotus team. Neither car featured in the Dutch Grand Prix, but

That brilliant victory run at Monaco in 1974. Ronnie holds his Lotus 72 tight into the apex of one of the hairpins

Ronnie revived their flagging spirits at the tiny Dijon-Prenois circuit a fortnight later when he beat Lauda to win the French Grand Prix. Niki led for the first ten laps before being slowed by a front end vibration on his Ferrari. I reckoned that Ronnie would have beaten him anyway and this proved one of the few times I've ever seen the Austrian slightly annoyed. "Look" he snapped, "I'm telling you it was tyre vibration or something in the chassis".

Ronnie eventually beat him by twenty seconds.

The British Grand Prix at Brands Hatch in 1975 will be remembered for many years to come, unfortunately not as a result of the racing though. In fact the race proved distinctly processional with Niki Lauda's Ferrari pulling increasingly further away from Scheckter's Tyrrell and Peterson, after a slow getaway from the front row of the grid, hounding Regazzoni's Ferrari. Lauda's Championship prospects looked pretty strong at this stage of the season. His Ferrari was fast and strong and he was driving sensibly and with a degree of mature restraint. Round the bumps and ripples of the Kent circuit, he found himself with a substantial advantage over his rivals and he never looked in any difficulty as he strode steadily away from them.

What happened in the closing stages of the race will be the source of much heated discussion for many years to come. Stuck's works March 741 crashed heavily at Dingle Dell Corner on lap 37, spraying the track with stones and mud. Within a few laps, several cars including Ronnie's Lotus dashed into the pits to change punctured tyres. It seemed that they were the result of running over all this debris on the circuit, and with just seven laps to go the eagle eye of commentator Jackie Stewart noticed that one of the rear tyres on the leading Ferrari was starting to deflate.

With six laps left to run, Lauda was in big trouble but still soldiered gamely on, ignoring the pleas from his pit to come in and change it. First Scheckter went past, then Fittipaldi. On lap 73 the rear tyre broke up completely and the Ferrari sagged onto the wheel rim. Lauda's plucky gamble had failed and he headed straight for the pits. The Ferrari mechanics replaced that wheel in double quick time, only for Niki to be faced with a wall of unauthorised people completely blocking the pit lane and preventing him from getting out to pass the timing line. It was a tragi-comic state of affairs which didn't finally resolve itself until just before the Canadian Grand Prix, the FIA eventually re-writing the results to give Lauda the fifth place that would rightfully have been his in the first place had he been permitted to drive across the timing line at the end of the pit lane.

The fact that Jacky had managed to bring his Lotus 72 through to third place, his best Grand Prix placing of 1974, provided little consolation for Ronnie who was now virtually out of the World Championship chase after a tenth place finish.

Next stop on the calendar was Nurburgring, that 14 mile strip of tarmac which twists and winds its way round the Eifel mountains in West Germany. The home of Germany's Grand Prix, Nurburgring puts a premium on precise driving as well as natural flair. Even though safety alterations over the years have improved the actual surface, they haven't reduced the number of corners to be negotiated, nor the fact that it can be raining on one part of the track and not on another. Just like Monaco, Nurburgring numbers amongst its victors most of the great drivers in racing history. On a slightly more sinister note, it has claimed the lives of many others.

In general Nurburgring hasn't been a lucky circuit for Ronnie. In

1972 he won the 1000 kilometres sports car race, sharing a Ferrari with his friend Tim Schenken. In the 1973 Grand Prix, his Lotus stopped with mechanical problems on the opening lap and a slight chassis failure in practice gave him a nasty moment on one of the fastest parts of the circuit although he managed to bring the car to a halt without damage.

In 1974 he wasn't so lucky. "This place isn't for me" growled Peterson as he arrived back in the paddock. Peter Warr hurriedly cleared a path through to the Lotus transporter, sweeping aside the hordes of photographers and journalists who were gathered to see Ronnie's damaged car. Eventually the huge German recovery wagon arrived, carrying the twisted remains of Ronnie's 72 like a broken twig on its back. Ronnie grimaced and climbed into the John Player caravan without another word. Warr diplomatically tried to throw a tarpaulin over one of the rear wheels which had broken round its centre. He didn't quite manage it and a dozen cameras clicked merrily, recording the cause of Peterson's disastrous shunt. The mechanics resigned themselves to a long night's work, grafting the rear end of the 72 onto the team's spare 76. It was funny how everyone was referring to the Lotus 76 now, even the Lotus team personnel, instead of JPS/9. A little cruel perhaps - when it was working it was to be the sponsors' car; when it wasn't, it was just a Lotus!

Ronnie had been lucky. His old Formula 3 sparring partner Howden Ganley lay in hospital at Adenau with two broken ankles, the legacy of a first lap shunt in the Japanese Maki earlier on Friday. The wreckage of the Kiwi's car was brought back to the paddock where Bernie Ecclestone was seen to look closely at the shattered car, pass a very amusing observation and walk away shaking his head thoughtfully. Everyone echoed his sentiments; Howden had been very lucky to get away so lightly.

Mike Hailwood was also a practice casualty. Just before the pits, his Yardley McLaren spun suddenly to the right and slammed into the barrier. Mike leapt out unhurt. Phil Kerr, his team manager, sprinted up almost before the dust had settled. "What happened?" he pleaded. "God knows" said a shaken Hailwood "it just turned right". Everyone thought that it was a most untypical thing for a McLaren to do, but the team examined all the front suspension wishbones on every car and beefed them up for the following day's race.

Race day dawned bright and the pundits predicted a close tussle between both the Ferraris and Fittipaldi's McLaren. How wrong they turned out to be. Emerson didn't quite get his McLaren into gear in time for the start and was rammed on the start line by team mate Hulme, both cars being rendered retirements immediately. Hulme, by now secretly decided in favour of retirement from racing at the end of the year, climbed into the team spare and set off from the pits. It was two laps before the organisers realised what was happening and black-flagged him. Denny waggled his finger at the man with the flag in mock self-admonishment as he crossed the line and couldn't stop grinning for the rest of the day!

Meanwhile Lauda, frustrated and on edge, reacted badly to being beaten off the line by Regazzoni and Scheckter. He lost his cool, tried to barge past Jody under braking into North Curve behind the pits and ended up slamming into the catch fencing. "Niki's really feeling the pressure" someone remarked as the crestfallen Austrian walked back to the Ferrari pit to proffer some explanation. Engineer Forghieri ruffled his hair jokingly. Nobody was too upset; he'd already won them a couple of Grand Prix races, so they forgave him his error!

Ronnie completed the first 14 mile lap in fifth place just behind Mass. Regazzoni, Scheckter and Reutemann were out in front and the Swede found himself embroiled in a hectic scrap with the German Surtees driver, Depailler's Tyrrell, Ickx and Hailwood in his second McLaren. For five laps he hounded Mass with a purpose and then noticed that it was Ickx in his mirrors, not Depailler. Little Patrick had tried to force a path inside Ronnie's Lotus as they came down towards the tricky Adenau Bridge about one third of the way round the circuit. "Ronnie didn't give me any room" Depailler remarked ruefully as his bent Tyrrell was pushed away. His only choice left was to glance off the guard rail.

Goodyear's Ed Alexander confers with Ronnie at Anderstoorp in 1974 as his mother and father (right of picture) watch over their son's progress

RONNIE PETERSON

By lap seven, Ickx had made his way to the front of the bunch. Ronnie somehow out-fumbled himself and ended up at the back of the queue but he wasn't giving up yet. On lap 11 Mass' brilliant drive in front of his home crowd came to an end when his Surtees' engine blew up, so that meant that the two Lotus drivers were left to fight things out with Mike the Bike. On lap 13 Mike made a heavy landing at the Pflanzgarten jump and his McLaren swung right into the barrier for the second time that weekend. Tragically this time he didn't get away unhurt, suffering a badly broken leg which was to keep him out of racing for the rest of the season. That left Ickx leading Peterson.

After the race, Ickx left the circuit without saying a word to his team mate. Coming round on the last lap, Ickx backed off quite noticeably as they approached the scene of Hailwood's accident where marshals were struggling feverishly to lift Mike out of his shattered McLaren. Peterson, a few lengths behind, backed off just a little bit less. It was all quite legitimate, but that extra few miles-per-hour enabled Ronnie to pass his team mate on the sprint up to the chequered flag. Ronnie pipped Jacky for fourth by just over a second. Ickx felt inwardly that Ronnie shouldn't have done it, but clearly decided against making an issue out of it. "I like Jacky very much" said Ronnie seriously later in the year "but he treats his driving as a sport these days. He's really an amateur driver nowadays who likes to drive in Grand Prix races".

From Nurburgring's twists and turns it was back to the wide open curves and sweeping turns of the Osterreichring. But this year there was no question of seeing the same sort of Lotus domination which Ronnie and Emerson had managed to stage in 1973. This time it was a straight fight between the Brabham BT44s of Reutemann and Carlos Pace and the two Ferraris. Back in his old Lotus 72, Ronnie ran gamely with the leading bunch and had actually moved into second place behind Reutemann's winning Brabham when, with eight laps left to run, a universal joint on a drive shaft broke. Ickx, relying on the Lotus 76 for this race, tangled with Depailler's Tyrrell and found himself out of the race three laps earlier.

There may not have been any reward for his efforts at Osterreichring, but Monza provided sweet solace for the whole team. After a host of practice problems, including a spectacular half-spin at Parabolica which wiped the car's rear wing off against the guard rail, the decision was taken to rebuild the car into the narrow-track trim which had been employed in 1973 when Lotus scored a 1-2 victory.

"That black car's there, look" remarked a colleague of mine as the field streamed past the pits at the end of the opening lap. Two Ferraris, three white Brabhams and then Peterson. That was the situation with Fittipaldi's McLaren right behind his old team mate. My colleague was right. It looked a long shot, but that black car was there all right. It all seemed a matter of simply waiting for the leaders to run into trouble.

Reutemann's Brabham fell by the wayside on lap 13, promoting Ronnie to third. Pace had dropped back with tyre vibration troubles and John Watson, driving the spare works BT44 after his private Hexagon car had crashed in practice, took an untimely trip up the escape road at the first chicane owing to braking problems. With 25 laps gone, all that remained in front of him was a pair of Ferraris. Lauda held his place at the head of the field, going like mad and pulling away every lap, while Regazzoni looked an equally comfortable second. It seemed inconceivable that Ferrari could lose on home ground. But they did.

To the disgust, the derision of the crowd, Lauda smoked to a standstill on lap 33 followed eight laps later by Regazzoni. Now 'that black car' led the race from Fittipaldi, the man now looking favourite to scoop the World Championship title. But Ronnie's Lotus was performing beautifully, its narrow track suspension arrangement enabling him to stay ahead of Emerson on the straight with little difficulty. And it's a brave man who dives inside Peterson on fast corners!

He was home and dry as long as he didn't make a mistake. Although Fittipaldi scrabbled past on one occasion under braking for the first chicane, Ronnie soon repassed and, knowing full-well the calibre of his opposition, beat the World Champion elect by less than a second in a carbon copy of his 1973 win. Emerson is a canny customer and, with that second world title almost in his grasp, he wasn't about to go sticking his neck out in a do-or-die last lap scramble with Ronnie. He knew his second place would bring him closer still to his second World Championship and that Ronnie was in no way a threat to that title. He simply sat there and waited. If Peterson should fail, then Emerson would win. If not, then no matter. The World Championship was the most important thing to the Brazilian.

Technically, if Ronnie won both of the North American Grands Prix and none of his rivals scored any points whatsoever, then he could win the World Championship still. But whilst outside bets do occasionally pay off in motor racing, such a fickle sport that it is, that was one hope that Ronnie realistically abandoned. There were too many good competitive drivers in strong cars vying for the Championship so Monza was virtually the end of the road as far as 1974 was concerned.

But Ronnie didn't give up trying. Two weeks later all the cars had been airlifted across the Atlantic and were preparing for the Canadian Grand Prix at Mosport Park yet again. The year before, Ronnie had been comfortably sitting in pole position, but now the situation was very different. Niki Lauda, the man Ronnie had predicted would be a top class Grand Prix driver way back at Rouen in 1971, sat firmly on pole position with his red Ferrari. The little Austrian was absolutely determined to salvage the World Championship title from the chaos and failure of his past few races. Alongside him was Emerson Fittipaldi's McLaren, so it was clear that all would not be plain sailing for the anxious Niki.

Champagne time - scattering the bubbly after his win in the 1974 Italian GP at Monza

Ronnie's fight with the Lotus 72 still left him a good way down the starting line-up, but he wasn't about to be disillusioned, and set about rectifying matters with a purpose the moment the flag dropped. His progress was absolutely electrifying. Whilst Fittipaldi chased Lauda for all he was worth, Peterson was fighting the opposition with a tenacity which even he had rarely exhibited before. With the odds loaded heavily against him, his progress towards the leaders was terrific. It seemed that nobody could stop him on this particular day.

German driver Jochen Mass, having his first drive in a works Brabham, was the first to feel the strength of Ronnie's challenge. He'd hardly seen SuperSwede in his mirrors before Ronnie was scrambling past up the inside, rubbing a front spoiler against his rear wheel as he did so. "I couldn't believe it" said a bemused Mass after the race, "One minute he was there ... and then he wasn't". In fact poor Mass was having a rather troubled time with his rivals; Andretti's new Parnelli closed the door on him going into one tight corner and obliged him to spin.

Unfortunately that damage to the front spoiler proved just a little bit of a problem. Once Ronnie tucked in behind other cars he found that he'd got virtually no downforce at all on the front wheels. "I was like a dragster" recounted a rather flushed Peterson once the race finished, "everytime I tried to apply full power going down the straight, the front wheels seemed to lift off the deck. Very exciting". But the problem hardly seemed to bother him. Within twenty laps of the finish he was into fourth place and charging after Clay Regazzoni's Ferrari like a hound after a fox. And it looked as though he might do it as well.

Poor Regazzoni really wasn't having much of a time round the bumps and ripples of Mosport. It wasn't that he didn't like the circuit, but he'd been caught out by a shower of rain during practice and done a lot of 'no good' to the front end of one of the Italian cars. He wasn't exactly flustered, but he certainly was susceptible to intense pressure. Less than ten laps from the finish, Ronnie started to close in on the Swiss' Ferrari and turn on the pressure. Suddenly the race looked grim for the Ferrari team. Lauda crashed into a barrier at low speed after sliding on some dirt thrown onto the circuit by another car, and now his Championship chances were gone for good. Only the presence of a slower car, coming up to be lapped by Regazzoni, saved the Swiss from relegation to third place on the last lap. Ronnie ended up in third place himself, possibly after the finest drive of his 1975 season.

It was now virtually certain that Emerson Fittipaldi would be World Champion for the second time in 1974. The issue at Watkins Glen lay between the McLaren driver, Jody Scheckter and Clay Regazzoni although the latter two would have to pull something very spectacular out of the bag in order to snatch the title. In the event, the United States Grand Prix proved anti-climactic in the extreme, the works Brabhams of Reutemann and Pace scoring a scintillating 1-2 triumph. James Hunt finished third with Fittipaldi, the new Champion, taking a rather disappointing fourth place. Neither Scheckter, Peterson nor Ickx finished the race.

It was a cruel contrast to the sparkling finale the previous year as far as Ronnie was concerned. It was a season of changing fortunes indeed and Peterson certainly did a lot better than the results merely indicate in recording those three Grand Prix victories. Success or failure, measured as it is by an individual's own aspirations, is an intensely subjective business. **145**

RONNIE PETERSON

Many Grand Prix drivers and several Grand Prix teams would have been head over heels with delight at the thought of equalling Lotus' 1974 Grand Prix record, but all it left at Hethel was a bitter taste of disappointment in the mouth.

Perhaps it was disappointment heightened by the fact that Fittipaldi's change of team had been so well timed. Certainly it was disappointment stemming from the failure of the Lotus 76 although that was largely owing to factors outside the control of the team. It seemed impossible that Lotus would drop to the depths of despair in which they found themselves during 1974. But they are not an organisation to wilt under the pressure of competition, nor do they wallow in their own self-pity. Lotus go motor racing to win and, as the 1975 season approached, there were already the faint murmurings about a new Formula 1 Lotus, a car personally designed and directed by Chapman himself with far less delegation than he allowed Ralph Bellamy.

But for Ronnie the hard reality behind the Lotus 76's failure was no compensation for a Championship lost. To start the year as favourite and then end up with fourth prize is an acute disappointment, just as to start last and finish fourth is pure elation.

Going into his sixth season as a Grand Prix driver, Ronnie Peterson took a brave decision. He put his faith where the results exist to back up the confidence of even the most sceptical. He signed another contract with Team Lotus.

About to give the author a quick spin round Brands Hatch in a Lotus Elan S130

CHAPTER 7
Where to next
Ronnie Peterson?

"RONNIE NEEDS THE same sort of partnership that Chapman had with Clark" said Alan Rees thoughtfully as he stretched out comfortably in a huge armchair, "Stewart and Emerson don't need partners". It was one week before the 1974 Brazilian Grand Prix and Alan looked more than usually thoughtful as we chatted in the spacious living room of his beautiful Buckinghamshire house at Hampden Row near Aylesbury. "Since he left March" continued Alan, "he's become so much more assured and experienced. Not just about racing, but in little things like buying an airline ticket. But he needs that partnership".

Ronnie and Barbro are very close friends of Alan and Debbie Rees. Even now he was with Lotus, Ronnie never forgot the support Alan had given him in those early years. Barbro spent a lot of time with Debbie. But it wasn't totally clear in those weeks of early 1974 why Alan was being so philosophical. It wasn't until almost a year later that it became plain what had been running through Alan's mind. Certainly Ronnie would have benefitted from such a close partnership. Whether or not he got it from Chapman or from Rees himself. Alan and Shadow team owner Don Nichols wanted Ronnie Peterson to drive for their team in 1975.

For many Grand Prix teams, 1975 looked like being the start of lean times. An increasing amount of restrictions on tobacco advertising, along with pressure from the Tobacco Advisory Council - an organisation which influences the way in which cigarette companies can advertise their products - made the way ahead for several sponsors look distinctly rocky. Even that great racing enthusiast Geoffrey Kent, Chairman-elect of John Player and Son, was obliged to hold back until the last moment in December before confirming his firm's continued links with Lotus for 1975.

In fact the problems beneath the surface were much larger than those that remained clearly visible. There would have to be a cut-back in John Player's financial involvement and there was even a period where the whole arrangement looked likely to collapse. But some hard talking between Colin Chapman and the powers-that-be at Nottingham ensured that this hitherto productive sponsorship arrangement would continue through 1975. Talks were held with both Ronnie and Jacky Ickx with a view to seeing just how

147

economies could be effected over a wide front. And all the time, the frustrated Lotus team must have realised that the Shadow team waited quietly in the wings with a large 'golden' offer. They wanted to buy that passport to Grand Prix success which was Ronnie Peterson.

Even before the Argentine Grand Prix in January the rumours swept like a forest fire through the International Speedshow at Olympia. Have you heard Ronnie's going to Shadow? Did you know they're swapping him for Jarier? No, they're swapping him for Tom Pryce? They're talking in terms of £150,000 for Ronnie's contract. He'll probably drive in Argentina. He's been to the factory and fitted for one of the cars. Pryce will drive a Lotus 72 ...

"I reckon the silly season is going out with a bang" smiled Peter Warr when I rang him at Lotus to put the inevitable question. "As far as I'm concerned, my drivers in Buenos Aires are Ronnie Peterson and Jacky Ickx". Warr spoke with a confidence in the matter which I, at least, found extremely convincing. So the next thing was a 'phone call to Alan Rees at Shadow's Northampton factory.

"Where did you get that absurd story from, I can't understand it". Alan replied with that air of concern which suggested that there was definitely no smoke without fire. I asked if Ronnie had been up to be fitted into a car. No comment, that was his reply. "As far as I'm concerned, my drivers for Buenos Aires are Jarier and Pryce". Even a call to Ronnie's Maidenhead home only elicited the reluctant reply "Oh, am I?" to the suggestion that he would drive for Shadow. If we were barking up the wrong tree it would be extremely embarrassing if we were quite wrong. On the other hand it was too serious a story to let go if it contained any vestige of truth. After a great deal of heart-searching amongst the editorial staff, *Motoring News* decided to risk it and splashed it all over the front page of the issue prior to the Buenos Aires race.

By the time we all arrived in Buenos Aires, the story seemed to be getting a little bit out of hand. An Associated Press telex quoted Ronnie as denying *Motoring News'* story but so many European journalists were now following up the story that it proved impossible to pin down just who started the ball rolling. By the time Thursday morning rolled round, the spacious foyer of Buenos Aires' modern Sheraton Hotel was crammed full of journalists, waiting hopefully for Ronnie's arrival along with Peter Warr.

However, Don Nichols beat them to it. Almost before his taxi stopped in front of the hotel we all pounced on him with the inevitable question. A diplomat to the core, Don merely smiled benignly and remarked "Well, that *would* be a good idea" in his deep drawl, considering every word carefully. Alan Rees waited patiently in the background like a loyal lieutenant. No, he couldn't say any more. It was up to Don. Clearly no change here.

Meanwhile, out at the circuit, everybody was busy asking why there was no name yet painted on the side of the brand new Shadow DN5, nor on either of the Lotus 72s. Peter Warr eventually arrived, worn out from his 14 hour flight from Europe and looking rather jaded to say the least. "I'm not making any more comments" he grinned half-heartedly "because they'll be misconstrued". Journalist Pete Lyons bounced up and asked a pertinent question. Warr answered almost automatically. "There you are" he quipped in a moment of frustration "I've done it again. I've made a bloody statement".

James Hunt, casually dressed in tee shirt and shorts lolloped up like a big friendly golden labrador. "Can you tell me who my team mate is Peter?" he grinned, thinking to himself about the press speculation which was also connecting Ronnie's name with a second Hesketh. "No, I can't" snapped Warr, by now tiring of the subject and almost asleep on his feet. "All I can tell you is that my drivers are Peterson and Ickx".

Why no names on the cars? Well, it was explained, Goodyear now monopolise the prime advertising positions on the rear wing side plates and so Duckhams have had to go on that little space behind the cockpit where the drivers' names were positioned last year. "In fact it's a bit of a problem to know exactly where to put them". As far as the Shadow was concerned, the explanation was that the car had been finished in a bit of a rush and they hadn't got round to pasting Jarier's name on the side. Had they got enough letters to spell 'Ronnie Peterson' to go with his specially tailored seat? Nobody offered a reply.

It seemed as though we'd all been wasting our time. Everything got underway at the start of official practice with both drivers in the teams their managers had assured us that they would always drive for. Whilst both Lotus 72s struggled with handling and braking problems, Jean-Pierre Jarier's Shadow DN5 proved an absolute sensation. By the end of Saturday afternoon, the new Shadow had comfortably annexed pole position for Sunday's Grand Prix. Carlos Pace was alongside him in the new Martini Brabham BT44B while local hero Carlos Reutemann in the second Martini Brabham shared the second row with Niki Lauda's Ferrari flat-12. Both Peterson and Ickx were well down the grid. Ronnie had a huge spin during practice and came back with a sheepish grin on his face. Mechanic Keith Leighton bent down and pulled handfuls of recently mown grass from the radiator scoops on either side of the Lotus. Chapman and Warr both laughed heartily at the incident, although it was laughter that disguised their concern over the cars' lowly grid positions.

It's now history that former Team Lotus driver and twice World Champion Emerson Fittipaldi won the Argentine Grand Prix in his McLaren M23. He took the lead after James Hunt's Hesketh spun on the hairpin before the pits and finally beat the gallant young Englishman by marginally more than five seconds. Peterson's Lotus gave up the ghost with dire engine troubles, possibly a broken valve. He'd been running hard on Emerson's tail in sixth place at the time. "But I'd not have kept up with him" admitted

RONNIE PETERSON

Ronnie, "I was just beginning to lose contact when the engine broke".

That evening Colin Chapman almost failed to make it to the Paris-bound plane. He left his passport at the Sheraton Hotel, but fortunately a messenger brought it out to the airport and found him there. I was last on the wait-list for that flight but *just* got the final seat. As we lifted off the end of the runway at Ezeiza airport late on Sunday night I half wished that I'd been able to stay over between the two races and talk to Ronnie again. Two rows further back in the Boeing 707 were Alan Rees, Tony Southgate and Tom Pryce. Rees had the stripped crownwheel from Jarier's Shadow, the stripped crownwheel which failed on the warming up lap. He was on his way back to Hewland Engineering for an explanation. I decided that this wasn't the time to start asking him whether Tom would be exchanged for Ronnie before the Brazilian Grand Prix, so I left them to try and sleep.

Looking back already to his 1974 French GP victory at Dijon-Prenois - here Ronnie demonstrates the art of the opposite lock

As for Ronnie, he didn't simply lie on a beach for the ten days between Argentina and Brazil. Later in the week he headed north for the United States where he tried a 3.5 litre BMW CSL at Daytona in preparation for the Daytona 24-hour race the weekend after Brazil. From there he went to Goodyear's Akron base where Don Nichols just happened to arrive at the same time. A neatly timed phone call from London to UOP's Chicago base confirmed that they would be taking publicity 'profiles' of Peterson to Brazil. And they would be printed on UOP headed paper. Just in case?

BMW 1-2. Ronnie leads Brian Redman round the banking at Daytona in the two 3.5 litre CSL coupes which contested the 1975 IMSA series. Ronnie shared his car with German rising star Hans Stuck, but engine failure sidelined them before the finish

Back in England, Tom Pryce consulted his solicitors and then let it be known publicly that he wouldn't move from Shadow to Lotus. The statement even got as far as the *Daily Telegraph,* so the next step was clearly a quote on the subject from Colin Chapman himself. After first trying to laugh it off as press speculation, he conceded that there was no smoke without fire but made it abundantly clear that he wasn't in a position to make any comment or statement yet "If any statement is to be made". Peter Warr had rushed back from South America to superintend the preparation of some revised rear suspension uprights for the two Lotus 72s to use in the second round of the Championship. Lotus were out to get back in business. Properly.

By the time we flew out to Sao Paulo for the Brazilian Grand Prix, the local papers were having a feast. It had virtually been decided that Peterson should drive for Shadow and there were plenty of photographs taken as Ronnie slipped into Pryce's old DN3 in the paddock garage. Still there was no official comment. Alan Rees, Peter Warr, Don Nichols and Ronnie went into conference at the Sao Paulo Hilton on the day prior to the start of official practice. The cloak and dagger atmosphere was sustained right up until mid-afternoon. Then Ronnie appeared in the coffee bar on the first floor where a group of us were waiting patiently for some positive decision to be reached.

"I'm on the move" he said, trying to supress a grin. "I'll drive a Shadow for the rest of the year". Everyone breathed a sigh of relief. At last, it seemed, the matter was settled. Several journalists slipped off round to the public telex office to tap out the news for European papers. If only they'd waited for a few minutes longer!

"You should have asked me" Alan Rees looked extremely angry. "I'm the team manager and I'll let you know who's driving the car". Less than one hour after Ronnie had happily appeared in the coffee lounge, the situation had been reversed. He would drive a Lotus 72 after all and the Shadow team remained unchanged. It was one of the few occasions on which I've seen Rees really angry. And it was the moment I fully appreciated that Ronnie Peterson was not master of his own destiny as far as switching teams was concerned.

Peter Warr looked as though a huge weight had been lifted from his shoulders when he emerged to leave for the track. On a thoughtful note he remarked to me "Do you realise, *if* Ronnie had left us he would have been the very first number one driver to leave Team Lotus without becoming World Champion". No, I thought to myself, I hadn't thought of that. But I could fully understand why Lotus, with their backs to the wall in one of the most difficult situations they'd found themselves for many years, wanted to hang onto Ronnie. If only they could keep him happy until the new car came on the scene, then they would almost inevitably have a winning combination on their hands again.

International Trophy 1974, Silverstone. Compare this shot of the Lotus 76 with the one on page 150 of the Lotus 72

Unfortunately the Brazilian Grand Prix turned out to be one of the worst races that Ronnie had ever experienced. Having complained about acute understeer throughout practice in addition to being landed with a badly misfiring engine, Ronnie hadn't his heart in the business after the car failed to fire up on the starting grid. He was almost a lap behind the field when he started the race and, after a few determined laps, he lost interest completely. He finished last, thoroughly despondent.

Jean-Pierre Jarier and the new Shadow simply underlined the promise they'd first hinted at in Buenos Aires. After taking the lead from Carlos Reutemann's Brabham on the fifth lap, nobody else saw them until they rolled to a standstill on lap 32 with the control arm temporarily seized on the fuel metering unit. "I've never seen that before with a Cosworth DFV ... ever" pondered Rees with an amazed look on his face. "Not ever".

Carlos Pace won the race, his first Grand Prix victory and in front of his home crowd at that. Emerson Fittipaldi's McLaren finished second, boosting his points total to fifteen with only two races complete. Ronnie slumped on a bench in the Lotus garage, not saying a word. Jacky Ickx, looking similarly fed up, sat opposite him. "Next stop bloody Daytona" said Ronnie thoughtfully, rolling the word 'bloody' round his mouth in a reflective vein. Barbro sighed; she had no wish to stay up for 24 hours watching anything!

Barbro's wish was granted shortly after the 24 hour race got underway. Sharing his works BMW with Brian Redman, Ronnie's car blew its engine after less than an hour's racing. The next day Ronnie and Barbro flew to Barbados with Dave Brodie, an English saloon racer, and his girl friend Kathie. Unbeknown to Kathie, there was a surprise waiting for her in that Caribbean island. Dave had arranged for them to be married. Ronnie and Barbro were witnesses. Dave spent the morning of the wedding trying to persuade Ronnie to marry Barbro at the same time. "No way, baby" said Barbro in mock disapproval when she heard of the suggestion although in her heart both Dave and Kathie suspected that she would have liked that. "Only a matter of time before Ronnie follows me" grinned 'the Brode' the following week back at Daytona. He was so right - Ronnie and Barbro were married six weeks later!

Ronnie decided to give Brode a treat after he'd married Kathie. "We'll hire a boat and I'll show you how to sail" he said with a mischievous grin. Brode said that he'd like that but mentioned as well that he couldn't swim. Ronnie said it would be alright if he wore a lifejacket. "I don't think he can sail at all" confided Brode to his new bride. He was about right there!

"I've done a lot of sailing on the Swedish lakes" explained Ronnie to the local native from whom he hired the boat". Brode tightened his lifejacket in mild apprehension. They started off from the shore and Ronnie immediately began fumbling round with the sails. "Then, by luck rather than judgement" Brode recalls, "he started off like a rocket after this fishing boat on the horizon. I'm shouting 'Ronnie what the hell are you doing' but all he does is laugh and keeps on chasing that fishing boat". Having gone so far out to sea that only the Barbados palm trees were showing above the distant horizon, Ronnie then contrived to capsize the wretched boat and all but drown the Brode in the process. "He's a bloody mad man" said Brode with a grin on their return. Ronnie couldn't stop laughing all afternoon.

Their holiday over, Ronnie, Barbro, Dave and Kathie returned to Daytona for the final round of the International Road Race of Champions. This event, enterprisingly organised by American team owner Roger Penske in association with Les Richater, had been organised over a four race series at Riverside, Penske's own track at Michigan and then at Daytona. The cars employed for this arduous task were specially prepared Chevrolet Camaros and the drivers who'd fought their way through to the final included just

Three weeks later; back on the banking at Daytona, this time in close company with Emerson Fitti-paldi. But this time the occasion is an all-Chevy Camaro International Race of Champions. It proved an exclusively American affair however, both Ronnie and Emerson spinning on the back straight

two regular European competitors; Emerson Fittipaldi and Ronnie. Other American drivers taking part were NASCAR saloon stars Bobby Allison, David Pearson and Cale Yarborough; former Can-Am champion George Follmer and past Indianapolis winners A J Foyt and Johnny Rutherford.

After some light-hearted practice during the previous week, the drivers drew lots to determine which car they would use in the race itself. The event took place over 40 laps of the banked circuit which meant that the evenly matched cars simply hurtled round in one great nose to tail bunch at speeds up to 165 mph. "I could weave from the top of the banking to the bottom and then back up again without ever feeling I was going to lose control" beamed Ronnie to Emerson once they'd finished practising. **155**

Emerson agreed that the specially developed radial ply racing tyres gave the Camaros an amazing degree of controllability. Whilst Brode and Kathie were thoroughly enjoying the spectacle of nine Camaros rushing around the banking, it was very clear that Barbro was not.

"When we're at a Grand Prix" she explained "I never worry because I'm so busy timing the cars. I don't like this, no, I really don't". It was unusual for Barbro to admit something like this and, although Kathie, Maria-Helena Fittipaldi and Kathryn Penske kept her company in the cool Goodyear hospitality tower, she carefully avoided watching the race's progress.

I must admit, I did see her point. If you don't acknowledge motor racing to be a hazardous sport, you must agree that it's pretty spectacular. And that IROC event was just about *the* most spectacular thing I've ever seen on a racing circuit. The cars started off quite gently at first with Ronnie and Emerson staying well to the rear of the group. In fact, at one point I was beginning to think that something was wrong with Ronnie's Camaro as he seemed unable to go for the lead at any time. Suddenly he proved us all wrong. In one lap he rushed low on the banking and sucked his way up from the back of the group virtually to the front. Fittipaldi did likewise. "Come on you bloody Brazilian" cried Maria-Helena to encourage her husband. She was as calm as Barbro was apprehensive.

"It's funny you know" remarked Kathryn Penske "but I took Barbro to see the IROC Camaros and just how well built and safe they are, but she really doesn't like this race at all". Every once in a while Barbro would raise her eyes cautiously from the floor and enquire quietly "how are they doing?" Then a grin would spread across her face. She realised her nervousness must have appeared a little on the strange side bearing in mind how many races she had watched Ronnie competing in. But she honestly couldn't help it.

Suddenly there was a huge pall of tyre smoke rising from the long back straight. Ronnie had spun into the wall, losing control of his Camaro as he dived out of A J Foyt's slipstream. "I tried to drive it away after the accident" Ronnie later admitted to an amused Peter Warr when he returned to England, "but it felt as if the suspension had collapsed". The truth of the matter was that he had punctured all four tyres as he spun at 170 mph, forcing his old friend Fittipaldi to waltz with him and plough up the grass on the opposite side of the circuit. Emerson eventually finished last, his engine down on power ever since he went spinning with Ronnie.

The race was eventually won by Bobby Unser from fellow former Indy winner A J Foyt. Both Maria-Helena and Barbro were relieved to see their men return unscathed to the Goodyear tower, although the way in which Emerson and Ronnie were laughing happily amongst themselves made them look like a couple of school children on a day out together. You'd never have identified them as the two closest rivals in Grand Prix racing today.

Then came the nicest touch of all. Kathryn Penske produced an iced cake and Barbro uncorked a bottle of sparkling wine. It was Ronnie's thirty first birthday. Everyone toasted him warmly and gave him a generous round of applause. And then they rushed off to catch their plane flights. The Fittipaldis home to Brazil for a few days on the beach before rushing off to South Africa for some Formula 1 testing. Ronnie and Barbro back to London with Dave and Kathie, Lotus' number one driver to discuss the season's plans with his team director.

Now all the haggling and doubt was over for good. Ronnie was to stay at Team Lotus, leaving Tom Pryce testing his new Shadow DN5 at Goodwood in preparation for the South African Grand Prix at Kyalami. A fresh Lotus 72 was built up for Ronnie to use at Kyalami but neither Peterson nor Ickx covered themselves in much glory. Ronnie finally started the race from the inside of the fourth row of the grid, bursting through into third place at the first corner only to fade during the race with dire handling trouble. Two days later during private testing the Lotus recorded laps almost two seconds quicker - the car ran with the same suspension settings and tyres as it had during the race. "I don't know, either" mused Peter Warr to that inevitable question - "why?"

Before the non-Championship Race of Champions at Brands Hatch. Ronnie rushed home to Sweden for a rallycross. Then it was back to Brands for an ironic third place finish behind Pryce's Shadow and John Watson in a Surtees. Then it was a spell at Silverstone testing a 72 as well as Formula 2 March which he was down to drive at Thruxton in the British Automobile Racing Club's Easter Monday International. A young Formula Atlantic driver Jim Crawford, was standing in for Ickx in the second Lotus. Unfortunately for Crawford a tyre deflated at the very fast Abbey Curve, pitching the 72 into a barrier and then rolling several times. Fortunately the car landed the right way up and Jim walked away unhurt. Ronnies' eyes bulged in amazement as he recounted the tale - Crawford appeared distinctly unruffled by the whole affair!

But something far more serious than a damaged Lotus befell the team the day before Crawford's accident. Peter Warr was involved in a very nasty road accident breaking both his legs, near Norwich, whilst on his way to the Silverstone, when his Elite was in collision with a Jeep which suddenly pulled out in front of him. Initial reports from his doctors indicated that Peter would be out of action for at least three months. With the new Formula 1 car still on the drawing board, one 72 severely damaged, Warr's hospitalisation seemed to be the final straw.

For Ronnie, the prospect of the Formula 2 race at Thruxton with an apparently competitive March - BMW looked like bringing a smattering of success. Ironically there was nothing but frustration waiting for him there. After qualifying in seventh place he collided with a slow Chevron which spun in front of him in the chicane. Before his March had stopped four other cars

157

piled into the debris. The instrument panel crushed down onto Ronnie's legs. For a moment he sat trapped in the wreckage thinking that both his legs were broken. Fortunately they were not; he was lifted gently from the car, examined by the doctor and pronounced intact. Dave Brodie drove Ronnie and Barbro back home to Maidenhead in his Bentley.

"I'm feeling really depressed. I thought Thruxton would give me a boost, but it just wasn't to be" Ronnie sounded very disillusioned although rather philosophical about the whole affair. 1975 had hardly opened on an optimistic note and all that lay ahead for the Swede after three Grand Prix races was the hope that things would get better. The strain on Ronnie's resilience, his acute sense of frustration, must have been intolerable. Would it affect his driving?

Probably not. Alan Rees had the last word on that. "Ronnie's too good for anything like that to affect him." Time alone will tell how justified Rees' confidence turns out to be.

CHAPTER 8
Frustration
and disappointment

NOT ONLY DID that Thruxton outing in the March provide another heartbreak, but there was similar treatment awaiting Ronnie when he arrived at Silverstone for the non-Championship International Trophy meeting two weeks later. The result of that event was to underline precisely who were the Championship contenders for 1975 and it made abundantly clear that Ronnie was a rank outsider with his ageing Lotus 72.

Despite his unfortunate testing accident, Jim Crawford was allowed to take over the other 72 entry at Silverstone. The decision to accept a second Lotus (most teams were allowed one car only) was in deference to their British sponsors, John Player, and, anyway, Jacky Ickx didn't seem unduly keen to take part. He too was starting to get disillusioned and, within three months, was to quit the team altogether.

There were some new suspension components on the 72 for this meeting and Ronnie was getting on with the job relatively well, qualifying third behind James Hunt's Hesketh 308 and the transverse gearbox Ferrari 312T of Niki Lauda, the man who would eventually go on to become World Champion. With a decent race in prospect, Ronnie's Cosworth engine blew up during the race morning untimed session. The mechanics sweated blood changing it, installing a fresh unit just in time for the start. But then came the final frustration. There was a dull metallic "clonk" as they fired it up and the new engine locked solid. Ronnie was out before he'd got to the grid and, with Jim Crawford crashing during practice, it seemed that there was no end to Team Lotus's plummeting fortunes.

The first European round of the World Championship took place in the picturesque Montjuich Park at Barcelona, but it was to be the last time Spain's classic road circuit would be used for their Championship qualifier. Pre-practice circuit inspection revealed the state of the protective guard rail to be very much less than satisfactory and the drivers, some say acting in high-handed fashion, boycotted practice. Only Jacky Ickx, no longer a member of the Grand Prix Drivers' Association, decided to practise from the outset although he was later joined by one other, the Italian girl Lella Lombardi in her March.

Most of the drivers spent the first day shacked up behind the smoked glass windows of Texaco's hospitality trailer, and although some work was carried out on the circuit overnight it was only in the second Saturday session that the drivers were persuaded to come out and practise. And then, they were only persuaded to do so when it became clear that the organisers were prepared to have all the racing cars impounded if their motor race didn't take place.

With all this drama apparently over, practice got under way on Saturday afternoon, but there was no way in which the Lotus 72 of 1975 was the same car Ronnie had used to dominate the Spanish Grand Prix before his retirement two years earlier on the same circuit. Instead of qualifying on pole he was back on the outside of the sixth row, fractionally slower than McLaren number two Jochen Mass.

The race was a much-publicised disaster. Fittipaldi boycotted the whole affair, flying back to his Swiss home before the race after driving round with his arm in the air during the final session of practice. Lauda and Regazzoni collided with each other going into the first corner, the two front row Ferraris rattling along the guard rail within yards of the start, so Hunt dived through to lead in his Hesketh followed by Andretti. Ronnie was way down in mid-field, racing along behind Stommelen's Hill and Pace's Brabham BT44B.

The mechanical carnage ran at a high level. Hunt lost his lead when he spun into the guard rail on oil dropped by Scheckter's blown-up Tyrrell. Andretti's

In the rain with the Lotus 72 during the 1975 Austrian Grand Prix at Osterreichring. Ronnie finished a morale-boosting fifth, despite a pit stop to change the visor on his helmet, but he might have been higher in the final order if the race hadn't been stopped at half distance

Parnelli "hit the wall" after its collision-damaged rear suspension collapsed; Watson's Surtees was delayed when the Ulsterman flat-spotted a tyre. Britain's two young hopes Tom Pryce (Shadow) and Tony Brise (Williams) collided with each other. Ronnie caught up to third place, hard on the tails of both Stommelen and Pace when he tried to follow them through the gap as they lapped Francois Migault's Hill on lap 24. Ronnie collided with the Hill car, bouncing his Lotus into the barrier and breaking a front suspension link bolt. Ironically, it was probably just as well.

If Ronnie *hadn't* retired at that point, he might well have become involved in the horrifying accident that befell Stommelen's leading Hill as it crested the hump beyond the pits on lap 26. As it went up the rise, the Hill's rear wing parted company with the car and there was the most monumental crash as Stommelen's machine flew over the guard rail into the marshal/photography area. Rolf survived with many broken bones, but four onlookers and a policeman were killed. Pace's Brabham went into the guard rail and was eliminated from the contest. Three laps later the Spanish Grand Prix was stopped and Jochen Mass declared the "half points" winner, the race not being re-started.

Monaco, where Ronnie and Barbro were soon to buy a flat, provided better luck for the Lotus 72. The race began in wet conditions and, from fourth place on the grid behind Lauda's Ferrari and the Shadows of Pryce and Jarier, Ronnie rocketed into second place by the end of the opening lap. Jarier, who'd taken second place as they streamed into the first corner, got so embroiled with shaking his fist at Niki's Ferrari in front of him that he drove his Shadow into the chicane guard rail on the first lap. That was his race run!

For the first few laps the leading threesome ran round together in tight formation, Lauda slipping and sliding his careful way a few feet ahead of Ronnie's Lotus while the willing Pryce watched with capable interest a few yards behind Peterson. Gradually this trio pulled away from the rest of the field.

As the track dried out so everybody edged into the pits to change their deep-grooved rain tyres for dry weather slicks. For one solitary lap, as Lauda was in changing tyres, Ronnie led the Monaco Grand Prix. Then he too stopped for fresh rubber. It was a slow wheel change and it dropped Ronnie to fifth when he resumed. Niki eventually won from Fittipaldi's McLaren and Carlos Pace's Brabham. Ronnie ended up fourth. Pryce, who was later to admit in an interview that he admired Ronnie tremendously and couldn't imagine anything better than being in a team alongside him, spun off and hit the guard rail.

Throughout the summer of 1975 Ronnie faded away as a challenger in Formula One. He appeared crestfallen and depressed most of the time, convinced that he could still do the job. The harder he tried with the 72, the less progress he made. Colin Chapman knew he wasn't the best test driver in the World, but also had the feeling that Ronnie could still perform well at the wheel of the right car. But Colin was embroiled with work on the boating and road car side of his organisation and, although he had prepared the concept of the "ground effect" F1 car by the summer of that year, it was to be the end of 1976 before the Lotus 78

RONNIE PETERSON

Proud father Ronnie with Barbro and their newly born Nina, 1975

appeared for the first time. Meanwhile, an interim design, the Lotus 77, was nearing completion for the 1976 season and the racing for the rest of 1975 would have to be conducted with the ageing 72s.

Ronnie's "Summer of '75" was simply awful. In the Belgian Grand Prix at Zolder something went wrong with his Lotus's brakes and he ploughed into the catch fencing at the chicane behind the pits. Lauda won. At home, in Sweden, he finished a frustrated ninth. Lauda won. In Holland he was running fourth a handful of laps from the finish when his car ran out of fuel. Hunt won, Lauda was second. In the French Grand Prix he fought a merciless battle with Jacques Laffite's old Williams to salvage a pathetic tenth place. Lauda won there as well. It was absurd to see one of the World's most naturally talented racing drivers groping in the dark halfway down the field with an uncompetitive car. And, to compound Ronnie's irritation, that buck-toothed Austrian lad who'd bought his way in alongside him as number two at March three years earlier, was now racing away towards his first World Championship title.

Just before Silverstone Jacky Ickx, who'd been having an even worse time as Ronnie's number two to the extent that *his* Lotus 72 had been blown off by Bob Evans's BRM at Zolder, decided to stop racing in Formula One. It was a mutual agreement between him and Chapman. They both publicly said nice things about each other, doubtless both relieved that they'd split up. For Silverstone it was decided to employ two young British drivers alongside Ronnie; they were Jim

162

Crawford (again) and Brian Henton, a bluff, likable Derbyshire man with an endearing brand of self-confidence.

Henton tested the Lotus for a couple of days at Silverstone prior to the Grand Prix, watched over by Peter Warr who was still on crutches but well on the road to recovery from the injuries received in his early-season road accident. Lotus were eager to recruit at least one British driver to their team, in deference to Chapman's patriotic streak and the fact that Chapman desperately needed somebody to set up the cars for Ronnie. They offered Henton a good deal for 1976. Brian declined, feeling he could do better elsewhere. He was diplomatic about the 72 at the time, but later told me "It handled terribly; I don't know how Ronnie drove it that quickly ..." Chapman later opined that Henton demonstrated one of the roughest styles he had ever seen!

The British Grand Prix promised one of the best races of the decade, practice ironically being topped by young Tom Pryce, the man whom Shadow had planned to exchange for Ronnie at the start of the year. The opening laps saw a sensational battle between Pryce, Pace's Brabham, the Ferraris of Regazzoni and Lauda and several others. But that tussle didn't involve Ronnie. Starting from eighth row of the grid, he lasted as many laps before his engine broke. The other two Lotus entries crashed later on, Henton during the sudden cloudburst that resulted in the British Grand Prix being stopped after 56 of its 67 laps.

John Watson joined Ronnie in the Lotus team for the German Grand Prix, again being politely non-committal about the 72 although he drove quite well in midfield. Ronnie's race was finished almost before it started when the clutch packed up and he came round the North Curve loop and straight into the pit lane immediately after the start.

The Lotus 77 at Interlagos during the 1976 Brazilian Grand Prix; Ronnie collided with Mario!

RONNIE PETERSON

Thankfully, in the Austrian Grand Prix a streaming rain storm at least allowed Peterson to regain some of his old confidence. This was another race to be prematurely terminated. But Ronnie found his old form and came flashing through the middle of the grid to hold fourth place behind Lauda, Brambilla and Hunt although he subsequently came in to change his visor and eventually finished fifth behind Brambilla, Hunt, Pryce and Mass. Henton, back in the second 72, crashed it badly in practice and didn't start.

And so the 1975 season staggered to a close for Ronnie Peterson. A fourth place in the non-title Swiss Grand Prix at Dijon-Prenois wasn't anything for the Swede to get excited about. Then came retirement at Monza and a certain fourth place in the Championship final at Watkins Glen lost on the very last lap. "I flat-spotted a tyre under hard braking", recalled Ronnie ruefully, "bloody James saw the gap and nipped through to beat me by a length to the flag ..."

Without any shadow of a doubt it was the worst season Ronnie and Lotus had experienced since the start of the decade. What's more, it didn't exactly take a clairvoyant to see that they were getting pretty fed up with each other. In a Christmas interview in *Motoring News,* Chapman suggested that Ronnie hadn't been giving as much of his effort as he might. "Ronnie, now, has all the flair and ability in the world, but he won't work at it", complained the Lotus boss. Peterson, fed up to the back teeth with the Lotus 72, simply sat quietly and waited for the start of 1976. The new Lotus 77 would be ready for him to drive in the Brazilian Grand Prix, so he would wait to see if that offered any improvement in his fortunes.

On the personal front, Ronnie at least could derive delight from one source during that troubled year. On November 4th, Barbro gave birth to their first child, a daughter whom they named Nina Louise. Little Nina's arrival was one of the few occurrences that brought the familiar Peterson ear-splitting smile to the fore once again!

The variable track/variable wheelbase Lotus 77 was unveiled in London shortly before Christmas 1975 and it was interesting that Jacky Ickx was invited along to be photographed in company with Peterson. Everybody was polite about the car, about its prospects, and it was gratifying to be able to record that John Player had renewed their contract with Lotus. They were to stay another three seasons as prime sponsors for Chapman's team, three turbulent years that were to see Colin re-establish his reputation as the most brilliant, innovative and successful racing car designer of his time.

It seems utterly amazing just how effectively Chapman managed that recovery when you look back on the 1976 Brazilian Grand Prix. Ronnie began his association with the Lotus 77 by crashing it in practice. Ronnie blamed the car, Chapman was inclined to think otherwise. Mario Andretti was recruited into the team for the race, although he was to do a couple more events for Parnelli before signing for Lotus full-time. Both cars qualified near the back of the grid and celebrated their first race together by running into each other. It was *that* sort of event!

That was the end of the road for Chapman and Peterson, or so it seemed.

Ronnie's March 761 leads the six-wheeled Tyrrells of Jody Scheckter and Patrick Depailler in the 1976 Italian Grand Prix. Ronnie won the race after a tough struggle

In the unloved Tyrrell six-wheeler at Interlagos in 1977. Ronnie was convinced, even after his second race with the car, that it was not going to work

RONNIE PETERSON

The loss of faith between them now appeared complete and complicated negotiations followed, before the South African Grand Prix. Over at March, Max Mosley and Robin Herd had now realised that Lella Lombardi's contribution to their efforts was never going to be worthwhile, so they sought to engineer Ronnie's transfer from Lotus. With financial assistance from what was described as "an overseas consortium" at the time (in fact, Polar Caravans and Italian Count Googhie Zanon, a great motor racing enthusiast in general and a fan of Peterson's in particular) the whole arrangement was successfully concluded. Part of the arrangement was that March would release their successful F3 champion Gunnar Nilsson from his F2 obligation and, after a few weeks' hectic bartering, the deal was done. Ronnie would return to March, Gunnar would go to Lotus.

It's fair to say that Ronnie's return to March seemed like a good idea at the time, but a number of factors prevented it from being quite as magic as many people expected. It was rather like trying to pick up with an old girlfriend after your marriage to somebody else had broken up. Circumstances were different. Ronnie wasn't the fresh-faced young kid that he'd been with them during his previous stay. He'd established himself as a Grand Prix winner and had now returned to see whether the 761 could lift him out of a depressing trough.

Ronnie made his *début* for March in the South African Grand Prix at Kyalami although that race was another disappointment because he was pushed off by Depailler's Tyrrell. He got involved in another tangle at Long Beach and it wasn't until Monaco that the old magic began to reassert itself.

Max Mosley recalls, "When he rejoined March in 1976 he was pretty well the same old Ronnie as a person, but he was much more philosophical as a racing driver. That last year-and-a-bit at Lotus had really demoralised him. He had become much more used to the fact that things *could* go wrong and he was more prepared to *wait* for things to go right.

"It was interesting, because he wasn't instantly quick in the March. It took until Monaco before his 'enormous go' characteristic began to reassert itself. You could always tell when Ronnie was trying because he came into the pits breathing really deeply. Peter Warr first noticed that and, whatever Ronnie might say, he wasn't trying unless you could see him breathing like that!"

At Monaco Ronnie chased Niki Lauda's winning Ferrari for 17 laps before spinning into the guard rail at Tabac after losing control on oil dropped by a rival car. He'd once again proved that he was quick enough to do the job. But the March wasn't a reliable car and, although towards the end of the season he qualified near the front of the grid in Austria, Zandvoort (pole), Monza and Mosport Park, the March would rarely last the distance. He led all four of these races, briefly, but only at Monza did things go right. After two years in the motor racing wilderness, Ronnie won the Italian Grand Prix again, fighting off an early challenge from the Tyrrell six wheelers of Depailler and Scheckter into the bargain.

Jacques Laffite qualified on pole position for that race, flanked by Scheckter's Tyrrell, while Pace's Brabham-Alfa shared row two with Depailler. Peterson's March was on the inside of the fourth row, flanked by Reutemann's

In the flame-spitting BMW 320-turbo during practice at Brands Hatch, October 1977

Ferrari and just behind the similar car of Niki Lauda. The Austrian World Champion was making a return to racing following a miraculous recovery from burns sustained in the German Grand Prix at Nurburgring six weeks earlier, another race which Ronnie had led very briefly with his March.

Monza was also the scene of a major row about fuel octane eligibility, a row which relegated James Hunt's McLaren and John Watson's Penske to the back of the grid following a dispute with the organisers. For Ronnie, who worked his way up to dispute the lead with the two Tyrrells, a shower of rain mid-way through the race came as a heaven-sent bonus even though it almost resulted in the race being stopped.

"There were a lot of reliability problems with that car, mainly surrounding the front tyres and brakes", Ronnie recalled two years afterwards. "That win at Monza was really very lucky because that rain shower just came at right time to keep the tyres cool enough. It was a cool afternoon, anyway, so we were in luck and I equalled the pole position time on the very last lap of the race".

For a long distance Ronnie squabbled with the Tyrrells, but they dropped away with engine problems, and Laffite began to press harder because Regazzoni's Ferrari was coming up onto his Ligier's tail. Then came the rain shower. Officials displayed the rain signal at the startline, intending that the race should be stopped, but Peterson just came past, his head cocked to the right as he looked at the man with the flag, and he kept going. He eventually held off Regazzoni to win with Laffite third (he'd eased up when he saw the official, think- ing it was all over) and Lauda a magnificent fourth in front of the Tyrrells.

167

RONNIE PETERSON

It was the victory that Robin Herd and Max Mosley had dreamed of ever since they started F1 racing in 1970. Not a washed-out, half length affair like Brambilla's Austrian win, but a full-length "proper" Grand Prix. And the man who'd won it was their dear old Ronnie. Sadly, it was too late. Peterson had committed himself to Elf Team Tyrrell for 1977.

"I didn't have any regrets about leaving March", Ronnie explained, "not even after winning at Monza. I really couldn't see any end to the sort of problems we were experiencing with the 761, that they would finally get on and do things properly. When I signed with them it was agreed that we'd do a lot of testing and in the event, we didn't. It wasn't money that was their problem, it was the difficulties they had trying to run three or four cars at once ..."

Summing up his old friends Robin and Max, Peterson admits that Herd has a lot of talent, "but he should spend more time on his Grand Prix cars. If he did that then he would be able to design a winner. Max? Well, he's a great businessman but I really believe he should concentrate on making money and not try to manage the team. He needs somebody else to do that".

Ronnie spoke those words twelve months after leaving March, sitting in the Elf motorhome at the 1977 Dutch Grand Prix. He was near the end of his year with Tyrrell, a year which was undoubtedly worse than anything March could have produced had he stayed with Mosley and Herd. It was all supremely ironic, but Ronnie could still smile about it all. Every time he referred to Mosley or Herd he would give them a good-natured verbal dig. Just as Max would occasionally lose his temper with Ronnie when he was driving for March and Ronnie would respond with that mournful look of outraged indignation!

Max's assessment of Peterson's move to Tyrrell is equally revealing. "I spent a lot of time talking with Ronnie about that, you know. In my own heart I just couldn't see that the Tyrrell six wheeler was the answer and it was certainly far too complicated for Ronnie to get the best out of. I'd always believed that if Ronnie was going to win the Championship with any team, then he either had to be joint number one with the man who was going to set the cars up or he would have to be given a car that was relatively straightforward to set up. Although, in fairness, he gave us quite a lot of feed-back from the 761 during his period with us, he wasn't in the same street as a Fittipaldi, Lauda or Andretti in that respect. No, I reckoned that the six wheeled Tyrrell was too complex. It wasn't his cup of tea. I tried to tell him this and I think he half believed me. Give Ronnie an uncomplicated car, easy to set up, and let him do the rest".

To grind through a race-by-race account of Ronnie's 1977 season with Tyrrell would be painful in the extreme. You can look in the results at the back of the book to see just how bad things were. His best placing was a third in the pouring rain at Zolder, a race won by fellow Swede Gunnar Nilsson in a Lotus 78.

Towards the end of the season he became almost desperate, hurling the six wheeler round with an abandon that was tremendous to watch, but which proved ineffective and began to cause some concern amongst his rivals. At Watkins Glen he nudged Nilsson off the road as Gunnar brought his Lotus up to

Helping Barbro into a miniature Grand Prix car at a track near Long Beach, 1976

pass the Tyrrell. "You pushed me off," said Nilsson indignantly. "I didn't see you, honestly", replied a subdued Peterson. Ronnie later told me that he'd persuaded Gunnar that he really *hadn't* seen him. "Bloody Tyrrell's mirrors", he growled in mock annoyance.

At Mosport Park, John Watson nosed his Brabham-Alfa alongside Peterson as they came into a right-hand turn. Ronnie ran over "Wattie's" nose section as he closed the door on him. At Toronto airport, Watson politely took the matter up with Ronnie. Later, on the plane, Peterson remarked, "If somebody comes alongside me into a corner, they're not past until they're level with me". John clearly didn't get much change out of this one. In Japan the season ended on a tragic note when Gilles Villeneuve ran over the back of Peterson's Tyrrell and launched his Ferrari into a horrifying series of somersaults that ended with a couple of onlookers being killed. Neither driver was harmed and this incident, most definitely, was not Ronnie's responsibility in any way.

The Peterson/Tyrrell relationship had been unproductive; a great disappointment, for each had held the other in high esteem. "I'd always wanted to drive for Ken," said Ronnie, "and I'd wanted to for a long time, I reckoned that they could not only give me a good car, but a competitive one as well. In the end the six wheeler turned out to be neither. It was far too heavy and unreliable".

Peterson reflected that he realised his plight within two or three races. "By the time we got to Long Beach I was totally convinced, although I suspected it wouldn't be any good as early as Brazil. In Argentina it almost cooked Depailler and I, it was so hot in the cockpits. We were almost dead in our cars and I spun off during the race through sheer lack of concentration". In Brazil, where there was a multiple pile-up on one particular corner where the track surface was breaking up, he simply spun off when a brake locked up.

"I touched the pedal and the car swapped ends", reported Ronnie. Pryce, following in his Shadow, reckoned Ronnie hadn't seen the pile-up and was amazed when he braked so late. That was Tom's last-but-one Grand Prix. Just over a month later he was killed at Kyalami.

The frustration of Formula One might well have been intolerable for Peterson if he hadn't been able to escape to the relative calm of touring car racing from time to time. In an era when top Grand Prix stars tend to confine their activities to the Championship trail and nothing else, Ronnie's enthusiasm for all other forms of racing was heartening. It was also very much a reflection of the fact that he simply loved racing cars and race driving.

Since 1974 he'd been linked with Jochen Neerpasch's BMW racing organisation and in the middle of 1976 they came up with an amazing "funny car", the 3·1 litre turbocharged CSL coupe which was intended to deal with the turbocharged Porsches in Group 5 category. It was only raced on two occasions in 1976 and both times Ronnie was at the wheel, sharing it with Gunnar Nilsson. In May they raced in the Silverstone Six Hours, but retired, while in early September they contested the Dijon Group 5 race with rather more promise. Ronnie qualified on pole position and staged a fantastic dice for the lead with Ickx's Porsche for the

Joking with fellow Swede Gunnar Nilsson at Long Beach, 1976. Nilsson was tragically to die of cancer only six weeks after Ronnie

first 40 minutes or so. Then the engine blew up again!

"It was a great laugh", insisted Ronnie, "but there was no way in which that chassis could cope with the power. It was a lovely car to have sheer fun in, but it wasn't a serious racer. It burned its tyres up like you wouldn't believe and you could spin the wheels changing gear on the Hangar Straight". His voice then lowered, "But I tell you, I came out of the right-hander before the pits at Ricard during testing and *passed* James's McLaren before we got to the Ess-bend after the pits ..."

Subsequent outings in the works BMW 320 saloons in German national races interested him rather less and he became really annoyed with Eddie Cheever when the young Italian-resident American kept driving into him at Nurburgring on one occasion. "That was just bloody idiotic", he complained. But his favourite **171**

RONNIE PETERSON

BMW was the 320 turbo, a good combination of speed and agility. With that machine he finished races rarely, but he loved hurling it around all over the place, giving spectators plenty of value for money. And the spectators loved him all the more for it!

But, flying back from Canada at the end of 1977, the relaxed and philosophical Swede wasn't thinking about BMWs any more than he was about the Tyrrell team which he'd just turned his back on. To the utter disbelief of everybody in the Grand Prix world, he was about to confirm the wildest rumours in the motor racing press.

For 1978, Ronnie was returning to Team Lotus!

CHAPTER 9
Back to
the top again

BY THE END of 1977 Ronnie Peterson could be regarded as a wealthy man. He'd earned a good deal of money up to that point during his professional racing career and, although only 33 years old, was regarded as one of the sport's elder statesmen. He had eight Grand Prix victories to his credit and, at the peak of his career in 1973, was regarded as the fastest man in the business without any question; faster even than Jackie Stewart.

From a personal point of view, his modest and well-ordered tastes enabled him and Barbro to enjoy a good life. They had a flat in Monaco and, in addition, they'd just purchased a beautiful country house near Cookham Dean in Berkshire. They were close to their old friends Schenken, Brodie and Ganley and, for the first time, Ronnie began to train seriously during the winter of 77/78.

Brodie, a fine athlete and a great physical fitness fan, cajoled Ronnie into this training programme. They mapped out a three mile route which was arduous to say the least, for the Peterson home was about 600 feet above sea level. It was a mile and half downhill for the first part of the run, then the same distance back; but uphill!

Brodie remembers, "I was almost pushing him with my hand in his back for the first few days but it wasn't long before he was doing it as a matter of course. It was a really hard route. You can imagine; running three miles in the country in the depths of a cold winter. But Ronnie was a fantastic, naturally talented athlete. I can tell you, I work bloody hard at my running, but all Ronnie had done was knock a ball around casually at tennis before that. And then, within five days, he was running as well as I could. That was honestly fantastic ..."

Ronnie was preparing for what promised to be the most successful season of his career. After months of careful negotiation, Peterson had forged another deal with Lotus boss Colin Chapman. Ronnie would re-join Team Lotus, nominally as number two to Mario Andretti. The press first got wind of this plan at Watkins Glen at the end of September, 1977, and it was clear that Andretti was cautious about the whole affair. Mario, looking at his third season as a full-time Lotus driver, was closer to a Championship title than ever. And, being a supremely realistic man, could see the potential pitfalls surrounding Ronnie's inclusion in the team.

Mario told me at Watkins Glen, "Ronnie had told me that he's quite prepared to come in under my conditions, but I don't think he should be doing this.

RONNIE PETERSON

He's a number one driver in his own right. But I'm insisting on certain conditions if he comes ..." For Chapman, the arrangement had tremendous potential if the sort of Peterson/Fittipaldi type problems could be avoided. For Ronnie, it was the chance to get into the most competitive car in the business and underline just how well he could still drive.

Peterson's devoted manager Stefan Svenby worked hard to assemble the contract that resulted in Ronnie's joining Lotus. Basically, personal backers (again Polar and Zanon, plus First National City Travellers Cheques) sponsored Peterson, and Chapman got himself a top-line number two driver at a substantial financial saving to Team Lotus.

"It was one step backwards to take two steps forward", explained Svenby after Ronnie's death, "and I think it was proved correct. He had re-established himself as the fastest driver in the business. The right team was more important to Ronnie at this stage in his career than the most money. Not that Ronnie was motivated by money. There were times I thought that he'd have signed a contract for five pounds if it meant driving for what he considered to be the right team! But seriously, being with the right team was the most important thing for him".

Ronnie first tested for Lotus just before Christmas at Paul Ricard in the South of France. Running both the Lotus 78 and the new, yet-to-be-raced 79,

Lotus mechanic Rex Hart stands by Ronnie's 79 in the pit lane at Brands Hatch, British Grand Prix, 1978

174

Ronnie quickly got into the swing of things and the two drivers were pretty well "even stevens" when it came to times. Mario didn't have as long with the 78, but Ronnie was new to it. 1978 promised great things.

The first Grand Prix of the season took place in the Buenos Aires autodrome in early January. The biggest threat to the established order came from the now Michelin-shod Ferraris of Reutemann and Villeneuve. But Andretti qualified on pole position and, thanks to Ferrari making a wrong choice of tyre, won easily. Niki Lauda finished second in the Brabham-Alfa BT45C, fractionally ahead of Depailler's Elf Tyrrell. Ronnie was fifth, troubled a little by blistering tyres, splitting the works McLarens of Hunt and Tambay.

Two weeks later the Grand Prix circus descended on the new Rio de Janeiro circuit, situated in coastal scrubland some miles south of the colourful, cosmopolitan Brazilian city. It was desperately hot and humid. Despite this, Peterson qualified for pole position ahead of Hunt, Andretti and Carlos Reutemann in the fastest Ferrari. But at the start of the race, Reutemann rocketed into a lead he was never to lose, confirming that Michelin were making tremendous progress in the world of Formula One. The Argentinian eventually won convincingly from Emerson Fittipaldi's Copersucar, Lauda's Brabham BT45C and Andretti, the American troubled with gearchange bothers on his Lotus 78.

Ronnie chased Reutemann briefly in second place, but had a coming-together with Villeneuve at the end of the long back straight. Both cars pitted for attention and, although Ronnie subsequently resumed, his car's suspension was damaged. It quickly collapsed, leaving Ronnie with a walk back to the pits during which he made his feelings clear to the still-racing Villeneuve. "I *wonder* whether he's got very good judgement", mused Peterson.

During the early season races, Ronnie's brief was to try the newly developed Lotus five-speed gearbox that Chapman was developing in his 78 on the first day of practice at each event. Problems repeatedly cropped up with his unit and it was always replaced with a regular five-speed Hewland unit for the second day of practice. Obviously that put Ronnie at something of a disadvantage because it cut down the practice time he had available to set his car up for a fast time. That happened at Kyalami where Andretti, running a Hewland gearbox from the outset, qualified on the front row alongside Lauda's new Brabham BT46, but Ronnie was down the grid on the sixth row.

The race was undoubtedly amongst the best of the season, initially featuring a superb race between Mario, Jody Scheckter, Lauda and the new Arrows A1 of Italian rising star Riccardo Patrese. Driving with an impressive maturity (which he'd have done well to demonstrate more often later in the year), Patrese moved confidently through these experienced runners and took the lead. He then motored steadily away into the distance, only to be thwarted by engine failure when he had the race in his pocket.

Lauda's engine blew up, Scheckter spun off and John Watson spun whilst running ahead of Peterson at the time. With ten laps to go Patrick Depailler's Elf Tyrrell had inherited the lead and Ronnie had pulled up onto Mario's tail, the Lotus

Ronnie and Mario, looking
pensive

78 running in second and third position. Dutifully, Ronnie didn't attempt to pass his team mate, although he felt that his car was a little quicker than Mario's on the straight. There, it seemed, the situation rested.

But no, four laps from the finish Mario came spluttering into the pits, his Lotus short of fuel. Chapman's fuel calculations allied to heavy consumption in that particular car, caused Mario to run short. Ronnie was through to second place.

It was a long shot, but Peterson pressed on. Going into the final lap there didn't seem any way in which Depailler could lose the race, unless something went wrong. Down into Crowthorne corner, the right-hander at the end of the long straight, Depailler came up to lap the private Lotus 78 driven by Mexican Hector Rebaque. Patrick went to pass on the inside of the corner, but suddenly television viewers all over the world saw Rebaque pull away slightly from the French blue car.

176

Depailler was in trouble with fuel pick-up problems. Suddenly Ronnie was alongside him. Round into the Jukskei kink they went like a couple of Formula Three cars, banging wheels through the right-hander at Sunset and down into Clubhouse. This was where Depailler knew himself to be defeated. Ronnie stayed on the tricky outside line all the way round Sunset which gave him the inside for Clubhouse. That, in turn, gave him the inside for the left-hand approach to the Esses. Depailler was beaten as Ronnie streaked back in the winner's circle after the finish of the year!

At Long Beach, the Lotus twins finished second (Mario) and fourth (Ronnie), while at Monaco neither of them finished the race in the points. Then, at Zolder, Colin Chapman's team reappeared with the Lotus 79, now fitted with a "normal" Hewland five-speed gearbox rather than the troublesome Lotus unit that Ronnie had been obliged to try in his 78 earlier in the season.

The history books will record that this was the first of four convincing 1-2 demonstrations from Andretti and Peterson, but while Mario controlled the pace of the race from start to finish in the 79, Ronnie was working a different kind of miracle with his 78. On lap 40, Villeneuve's Ferrari staggered into the pits with a shredded front tyre. The little French Canadian driver had been the only man to keep Mario remotely in sight and his misfortune promoted Ronnie's 78 to second place. It looked like an easy Lotus landslide.

Then, near disaster. Ronnie came hurtling into the pits for fresh front rubber at the end of lap 57. His left front tyre was worn down by the pace of the race, so two fresh covers were slammed on and Ronnie went boiling out into the fray once more. On lap 63 he forced his way past Laffite's Ligier with a vengeance to take back third place, but Reutemann's second place Ferrari was over six seconds in front of him with seven laps to go. Troubled with gear selection bothers, there was no way in which "Lole" was a match for Ronnie's speeding Lotus. Just three laps later Ronnie was on his tail, then through and away to finish a storming second with the race's fastest lap (unsurprisingly) to his credit.

This marked the start of Ronnie's most successful summer. He was second at Jarama, first time out at the wheel of *his* Lotus 79, despite an appalling start. He was third, after a pit stop and some bad baulking from Patrese, at Anderstorp. Then he was second again, a whisker behind Mario, at Paul Ricard. Pole position at Brands Hatch followed, but both Lotus 79s retired from the race, while he led the opening stages at Hockenheim only to drop out whilst running second shortly before the end when a gearbox bearing began breaking up.

Of course, his greatest day was in Austria where he led the re-started Grand Prix at the Osterreichring virtually from start to finish. It was a brilliant virtuoso performance which saved Team Lotus's fortunes after Andretti spun into the guard rail coming out of the first corner of the prematurely terminated first race. The first event began in dry, but slippery, conditions and was stopped after only seven laps when the heavens opened. The re-start took place on wet weather tyres and, as the circuit dried out, the field stopped to change back onto slicks. But Ronnie simply vanished into the distance to win his second Grand Prix of the season by a contemptuous margin from Depailler's Tyrrell and the promising Villeneuve in his Ferrari.

But without doubt the most convincing display of Lotus might came at Zandvoort, in the Dutch Grand Prix, two weeks before Ronnie's death. Mario and Ronnie started from side to side on the front row of the grid, took the lead into the first corner and ran away from the field in close, tight 1-2 formation. Niki Lauda made a brave effort to get on terms with them, but his Brabham-Alfa was no match for the 79s, even though Mario's car had a broken exhaust and Ronnie's rear brakes were failing badly towards the end of the event.

The Monza tragedy brutally tore asunder a productive, close relationship between Chapman, Andretti and Peterson, although Ronnie had already made the decision that he would not be driving for Lotus in 1979. It was an enormously difficult choice for him to make, for he wasn't shuffling out dejected, in the middle of a season as he had been in 1976. Peterson and Chapman had a high regard for each other, appreciating each other's strong points as well as idiosyncrasies. More so than March, Lotus was Ronnie's spiritual home as far as motor racing was concerned.

"There's certainly no doubt of that in my mind", said Svenby, "Colin really

Talking to McLaren team manager Alistair Caldwell in the pit lane at Monza, Sunday, September 10, 1978

The last Andretti-Peterson 1-2 finish. Mario and Ronnie, their Lotus 79s in tight formation during the 1978 Dutch Grand Prix at Zandvoort

reckoned him". As for Ronnie himself, standing in the paddock on the morning of the Dutch Grand Prix he summed up his feelings by saying, "He may be difficult and hard at times, but Colin's the best team manager, designer and boss. The best". After a pause he added "My God, and *how* he's the best". Yet, almost within hours, Peterson was to turn his back on Lotus and opt for McLaren in 1979. Why?

One can appreciate the dilemma facing both Chapman and Ronnie. The combination of Andretti, Peterson and the Lotus 79 was altogether too good to be true. It was Andretti, with his single-minded application, sensitive ability as a test driver and dogged determination, who'd helped make the 79 the effective car it was. He was close to his World Championship title and, realistically, there was no way he could be deprived of it. Ronnie had pledged himself to help Mario win, even at his own expense. Mario hadn't got to worry about his team mate. But could one reasonably expect Mario Andretti, the 1978 World Champion driver, to take Ronnie on as joint number one, equal in all respects, for 1979?

Obviously one might ask him, but nobody was surprised when Mario proved less than enthusiastic about the prospect. Andretti is a highly intelligent individual and didn't want to get pushed into the same position as Fittipaldi had been in 1973. Set the car up, painstakingly, then have Ronnie go a second a lap faster with the same set-up. He was quite prepared to face Peterson on equal terms, but he wanted those equal terms to come from within different teams. It's significant that about the only news that lit up Mario's face with a smile after the race finished at Monza was the premature information about Ronnie's condition. When somebody mentioned the fact that Ronnie would be able to race his new McLaren by the start of the European season, Mario was delighted by the news. It was sadly optimistic.

However, it can never be emphasised sufficiently that Ronnie's gamble had paid off. He had re-established himself as the fastest man in the business, even though there was still this question mark over his ability as a test driver. But, after examining all the options open to him, he decided that McLaren would be the best place to go. The Colnbrook-based team had sacrificed success in 1978 in order to do the best possible job on their ground effect car, the McLaren M28. If anybody could follow the lead set by Chapman, everybody reckoned McLaren would probably do the best job based on past experience.

Right to the end, Chapman tried to get the two drivers to run together once more. At Zandvoort it became clear that he could juggle things no more. Ronnie was moving on. Chapman wanted him to stay with the team, long term, on the basis that he'd "moved round enough; now settle down at home where you belong". At any rate, it was better to have Ronnie at Lotus rather than racing against the 79s in a really good rival car. One also considers Jackie Stewart's oft-quoted thesis that once a driver wins his Championship title, he subconsciously relaxes very slightly, this "relaxation" often extending through to the following season. Perhaps, allowing for that characteristic showing itself in Mario's case, could Ronnie have snatched a Championship from his team mate in 1979? We shall never know.

Chapman and the Lotus lads leap for joy as Ronnie sweeps across the line to win the 1978 Austrian
Grand Prix, the final win of his career

RONNIE PETERSON

Reflecting on the 1978 season of Lotus dominance, one can recall occasions when Ronnie really let Mario know of his true driving capabilities. At Rio, when Ronnie qualified on pole, Mario was a trifle cool. At Brands Hatch Ronnie sat in the pit lane, having qualified for pole on hard tyres, while Mario tried to match his time on qualifiers. Perhaps significantly, that was the only time Ronnie ever praised his own efforts. "The man who's on pole at Brands Hatch is a bloody good driver", he growled to Dave Brodie afterwards. Then again at Hockenheim, Ronnie jumped into the lead at the start and gave it everything he'd got for the first six laps. When Andretti went past, it was *really* close stuff. "I thought, I'm not talking to you today", smiled Mario when the race had finished. Finally, at Zandvoort, Ronnie came up alongside at the chicane once or twice, "Just to let Mario know I was there. I kept seeing Niki's Brabham in my mirrors and I didn't like that at all!"

Happily, on a personal basis the two team mates matured into firm friends and spent an enormous amount of time in each other's company away from the circuits. After Ronnie's death, Mario reaffirmed, "I was really looking forward to racing him in that McLaren next year. Racing our asses off and then sitting down to talk about it over a beer. That's what's so wonderful about this business if you can have that sort of relationship with a person".

Few people doubted he was being anything else than utterly genuine in his sentiments.

CHAPTER 10
Monza

AFTER A DISAPPOINTING outing with the works BMW 320 turbo in the Group 5 sports car race at Vallelunga, the circuit on which he'd clinched his European F2 Championship seven years earlier, Ronnie flew back to Monaco for a couple of days and then off to Monza. Barbro stayed in their flat on the Mediterranean coast, recovering from a recent miscarriage. The arrangement for Ronnie to join McLaren Racing was now finalised and, indeed, Carlos Reutemann had been signed as joint number one at Lotus for 1979. The "grand alliance" had finally split up for good.

Prior to Monza there was no way in which Mario Andretti could be beaten to the World Championship title unless it was by Ronnie. The American ace had amassed a total of 63 points to Ronnie's 51 points. Niki Lauda, a hard-driving third at Zandvoort, had a total of 35 points. Even if Niki won in Italy, the USA and Canada, his points total would only be boosted to 62 points, so he would still end up one short of retaining his title. And, as Ronnie had pledged himself to assisting his team mate, Andretti's title was assured come what may.

For Ronnie and Team Lotus, Monza held mixed memories. For Chapman's team there was joy mingled with sadness. Monza was the place where Jim Clark had been involved in the terrible accident which killed Wolfgang von Trips and a crowd of spectators back in 1961. Nine years later Jochen Rindt died at the wheel of a Lotus 72 but, on a happier note, Emerson Fittipaldi clinched his first Championship title at Monza in 1972. What's more, Ronnie won the race for Lotus in both 1973 and 1974, ironically beating Fittipaldi's McLaren in the latter race. Ronnie grinned as he recalled winning the 1976 race in the March 761. "If it hadn't been for that rain shower", he grinned, "we'd have never kept its front tyres in one piece ..."

For Monza, as usual, there were four Team Lotus machines available. Andretti, as number one, exercised his usual monopoly over the use of 79/4 and 79/1, the former being his designed race car. Peterson, again as usual, had his regular 79/2 with faithful old 78/3 as his back-up machine. Since Mario's first lap accident at Osterreichring there were only three 79s regularly available.

From the outset at Monza, everything went wrong for Ronnie. The two 79s edged out into the hectic traffic of the first practice session as usual, but whilst Andretti roared away to a best of 1 minute 37.780 seconds, the quickest in the session, Ronnie was soon coasting back up the pit lane. He stopped a few yards short of his allocated pit, so Rex and Bobby ran down to push him in. Ronnie undid the harness and stepped out in disgust. Nigel Bennett looked into the injection trumpets and winced as he saw fragments of metal. The engine had blown up in a big way, so Ronnie climbed onto the pit counter and immersed himself in reading the current copy of *Autosport* in which was a lengthy article about him under the heading "Supersecond", a title alluding to the way he'd played 'white man' all season long.

Was he going out in the 78? "No, I'll just set pole tomorrow", he grinned rather sheepishly. Nevertheless, the Lotus lads wheeled 78/3 out into the pit lane at the start of the second session and Ronnie had a short spell at its wheel. His best was 1 minute 40.518 seconds; nowhere near his best in the 79 before its engine blow-up which had been good enough to stand him in second quickest behind Mario.

"Give him a taste of what he'll be driving next year", joked one of the Lotus mechanics. Everybody smiled. The new McLaren M28 was due to test just over a week after Watkins Glen and nobody doubted that Ronnie would be a strong force to be reckoned with in 1979. Rex and Bobby thumbed their way through the week's motoring magazines, asking "*Is* Reutemann coming to us?" with a concerned look on their faces. Not that they'd got the slightest objection to Carlos; they'd just been hoping that Ronnie would stay with them.

A fresh engine was installed in Ronnie's car ready for the untimed practice session on Saturday morning. But still things weren't right. Within a few laps he was back in the pit lane, quietly fuming behind his face mask as Bobby crouched under the Lotus's back end examining the brakes. "The pads aren't clearing the discs properly", he said thoughtfully, "there must be a valve sticking somewhere in the system".

By the end of the session there were even more problems. Nigel walked across to Chapman and whispered into his ear. The Lotus boss's face contorted briefly; "I thought we'd cured that sort of thing", he shrugged. A gearbox oil seal had failed and lubricant was leaking down onto the clutch. The 79 was pushed away again, but this time Ronnie didn't bother with running the 78 in the afternoon session. Ten minutes from the finish his 79 was wheeled back into the pit lane, he was strapped in and roared out onto the circuit. Five laps later the chequered flag fluttered and practice was over. Ronnie hadn't had time to improve on his Friday time. He would start the Italian Grand Prix from the inside of the third row, fifth fastest overall. Ahead of him would be his team mate Andretti, Gilles Villeneuve's Ferrari, Jabouille's Renault and the Brabham-Alfa Romeo of his old friend Niki Lauda. Alongside him on the third row, a fraction slower than his Lotus, would be Alan Jones in the Frank Williams car.

Race day produced the customary chaos at Monza, with thousands of enthusiastic fans pouring in from an early hour. The accessory and model stalls were doing a roaring trade and easily the most popular 'buy' was the scale model of the Lotus 79, complete in its John Player/Olympus livery. The drivers sought the peace and cool of their motorhomes until it was time to go out for the half-hour warm-up.

After a few laps, Ronnie didn't come round. His 79 had crashed at the second chicane, ploughing through layers of catch fencing and running head-long into the barrier. Ronnie, his legs slightly bruised, walked back to report that the "... bloody brakes were playing up again". After the warm-up was over, the damaged 79 was returned to the paddock by one of the breakdown trucks. There was no way in which it was going to be repaired in time for the start, so the mechanics resigned themselves to preparing 78/3. Ronnie returned to the Lotus motorhome, looking thoughtful, and sat talking with Andretti.

The start at Monza was scheduled for 3.30 in the afternoon, but drivers and cars were in the pits the best part of an hour before than. Young Villeneuve, on the front row in his Ferrari, looked more pensive than usual. The weight of the world was obviously on his shoulders; 26 years old and carrying the responsibility for Italian honour in front of a Monza crowd. Quite a lot to ask of this relative novice in the F1 firmament.

Eventually they eased out of their warming-up lap and returned to sit motionless on the wide Monza apron as mechanics busied themselves with final checks and adjustments. Then they were away on their pace lap, weaving from side to side to warm-up their tyres to working temperatures. Ever so gently they came back out of Parabolica and eased up towards their grid positions. The front few rows were just stationary when the starter switched the lights from red to green.

Villeneuve made a magnificent getaway, beating Mario off the line fair and square, but behind these two chaos reigned. The back half of the grid, still moving when the starting signal was given, made full use of their ready-made advantage and swamped everybody in front. Riccardo Patrese and Vittorio Brambilla roared away down the right-hand side of the pack, to be faced by serious problems as they tried to funnel back into line at the point where the startline straight narrows to half its maximum width, the section that leads into the first chicane.

Ronnie's Lotus made a relatively tardy start from the third row of the grid. Suddenly, about 300 yards away from the start, cars began to tangle with each other and Ronnie's 78 came into violent collision with another car, probably Hunt's McLaren, which had been pushed into the Lotus by a third machine. The Lotus crashed nearly head-on into the angled guardrail which blanks off the entrance to the disused banked circuit, the front end was ripped off and the car exploded in flame as fuel lines were severed. Then the blazing machine cannoned back across the circuit and suddenly cars were going everywhere. Hunt's McLaren, Reutemann's Ferrari, Daly's Ensign, Lunger's McLaren, the Shadows of Stuck and Regazzoni, the Tyrrells of Depailler and Pironi and Brambilla's Surtees were all involved and crashed to a chaotic halt.

With great presence of mind, James Hunt leapt from his stationary McLaren and tore back up the track to the blazing wreck of Ronnie's Lotus. Without a second thought, he kicked the release button on Ronnie's harness and **185** dragged the Swede, conscious but white with pain from two badly broken legs, out of the wreckage with the help of Clay Regazzoni. A very prompt and capable fire marshal doused the flames as best he could, but the more immediate problem was to get Ronnie into an ambulance. After an unnecessary delay, an ambulance arrived and he was whisked away by helicopter to the Niguarda Clinic.

Vittorio Brambilla, unconscious following a blow on his head from a flying wheel, was also removed to hospital, while Hans Stuck suffered from delayed shock a short while afterwards and was unable to take part in the re-start.

Three hours later, after argument and debate, the race was eventually re-started over a reduced distance of 40 laps. Andretti and Villeneuve were both penalised for blatant, but understandable, jump starts and thus victory went to Niki Lauda's Brabham-Alfa. Not a triumph savoured by the Austrian in any way, shape, or form.

At the hospital it appeared that Peterson, although suffering badly from shock, would survive. Word came back to the circuit to the effect that, although his legs were badly broken, he would pull through and make a complete recovery. Andretti, completely drained from the day's events and unable to comprehend that he was now World Champion, raised a smile for the first time since the race on hearing that news. He couldn't wait for Ronnie to recover and get into his new McLaren. He was really looking forward to sorting out who was the best in 1979!

Within a matter of hours, the situation changed dramatically. After a lengthy operation to set his shattered legs, it became clear that complications were arising. Ronnie's circulation was becoming impaired as bone marrow embolisms got into his bloodstream. By the early hours of Monday morning, he was reported as being "in a deep coma" and the surgeon responsible for his treatment opined that "Only a miracle will save him". But there were to be no miracles on Monday, September 11th. By breakfast time the news was being flashed round the world. Ronnie Peterson was dead.

A helicopter had been sent down to Nice to collect Barbro and bring her to Ronnie's side. Owing to fog, she arrived late at Milan's Malpensa airport where Stefan Svenby met her with the terrible news. Shattered, she didn't leave the plane and was immediately flown home to stay with her relatives in Sweden. Andretti, broken up by the news of his team mate's death, spoke of the day that should have been the happiest of his whole life turning into the most miserable. Everybody in Grand Prix racing was shocked beyond words.

The story was over. Four days later they buried Ronnie in his home town, Orebro. From all over Europe came his friends and rivals to join Barbro in paying their last respects in the Cathedral of St. Nicolas. Niki Lauda, John Watson, James Hunt, Jody Scheckter, Emerson Fittipaldi, Gunnar Nilsson, Tim Schenken, Teddy Mayer, Colin Chapman, Ken Tyrrell, Frank Williams, Dave Brodie, Alan Rees, Bernie Ecclestone and hundreds of other friends and fans were present. Mario, sadly, was unable to obtain a release from his USAC team to be present, as he was committed to a race that weekend.

"Ronnie wasn't cast in the popular image of a racing driver. He was a gentle, quiet man who loved his family". Those were the words of Colin Chapman in a television tribute to Ronnie a few days after the accident. Simple sentiments, but ones which summed up the feelings of people who knew Ronnie Peterson and loved him for those and so many other qualities he possessed.

Ronnie Peterson and Barbro Edvardsson at their wedding at Maidenhead in April 1975

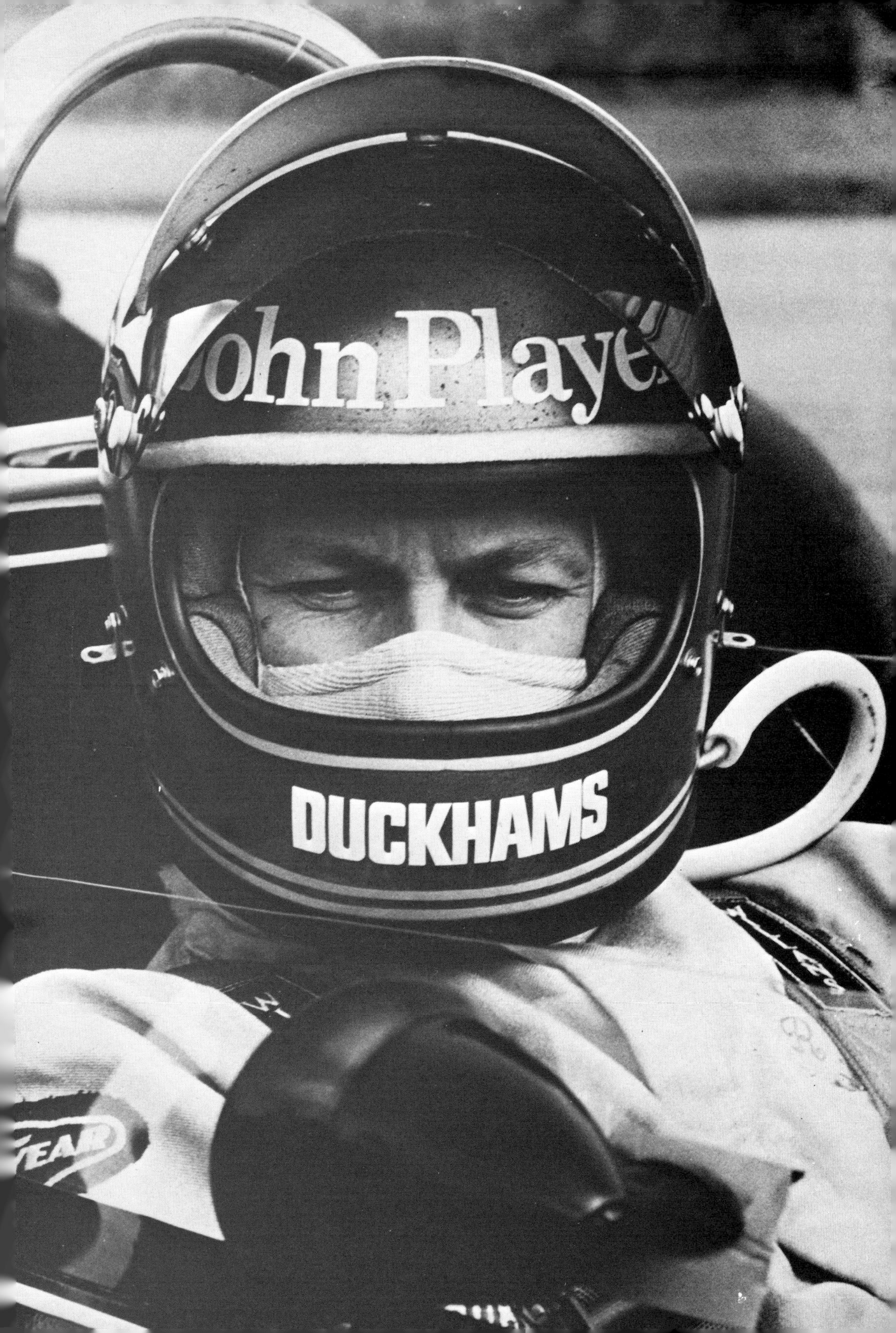
DUCKHAMS

Race results

1970

April 26	F2 Barcelona	March 702	Retired
May 3	F2 Nurburgring	March 702	Retired
May 10	**MONACO GP**	**March 701**	**7th**
May 24	F2 Zolder	March 702	Retired
May 25	F2 Crystal Palace	March 702	Crashed
June 7	**BELGIAN GP**	**March 701**	**Retired**
June 14/15	Le Mans 24 hours	Ferrari 512 (with Derek Bell)	Retired
June 21	**DUTCH GP**	**March 701**	**Retired**
June 28	F2 Rouen	March 702	6th
July 18	**BRITISH GP**	**March 701**	**8th**
July 26	F2 Paul Ricard	March 702	6th
Aug 2	**GERMAN GP**	**March 701**	**Retired**
Aug 30	F2 Mantorp Park	March 702	Retired
Sept 6	**ITALIAN GP**	**March 701**	**Retired**
Sept 13	F2 Tulln Langenlebarn	March 702	5th
Sept 19	**CANADIAN GP**	**March 701**	**14th**
Sept 26	F2 Imola	March 702	4th
Oct 4	**UNITED STATES GP**	**March 701**	**11th**
Oct 11	F2 Hockenheim	March 702	3rd

1971

March 6	**SOUTH AFRICAN GP**	**March 711**	**Retired**
March 14	F2 Mallory Park	March 712	Crashed
March 21	F1 Race of Champions	March 711	Retired
March 28	F1 Questor GP	March 711	18th
April 4	F2 Hockenheim	March 712	Retired
April 12	F2 Thruxton	March 712	2nd

April 18	**SPANISH GP**	**March 711**	**Retired**
April 25	F2 Pau	March 712	Retired
May 2	F2 Nurburgring	March 712	Retired
May 8	F1 Silverstone	March 711 (Alfa)	Crashed
May 16	F2 Jarama	March 712	Retired
May 23	**MONACO GP**	**March 711**	**2nd**
May 31	F2 Crystal Palace	March 712	3rd
June 5	2 litres Martini Trophy	Lola T212	2nd
June 20	**DUTCH GP**	**March 711**	**2nd**
June 27	F2 Rouen	March 712	1st
July 4	**FRENCH GP**	**March 711 (Alfa)**	**Retired**
July 17	**BRITISH GP**	**March 711**	**2nd**
July 24	Watkins Glen 6 hours	Alfa-Romeo T33-3	1st
		(with Andrea De Adamich)	
August 1	**GERMAN GP**	**March 711**	**5th**
August 8	F2 Mantorp Park	March 712	1st
August 15	**AUSTRIAN GP**	**March 711**	**8th**
August 22	F2 Kinnekulle	March 712	1st
August 30	F2 Brands Hatch	March 712	1st
Sept 5	**ITALIAN GP**	**March 711**	**2nd**
Sept 12	F2 Tulln Langenlebarn	March 712	1st
Sept 19	**CANADIAN GP**	**March 711**	**2nd**
Sept 26	F2 Albi	March 712	5th
Oct 3	**UNITED STATES GP**	**March 711**	**3rd**
Oct 10	F2 Vallelunga	March 712	1st
Oct 11	2 litre Barcelona ì	Lola T212	1st
		(with Jo Bonnier)	
Oct 24	F1 Brands Hatch	March 711	16th
Oct 31	F2 Interlagos	March 712	2nd
Nov 7	F2 Interlagos	March 712	10th
Nov 14	F2 Porto Alegre	March 712	Retired
Nov 21	F2 Cordoba	March 712	Retired

1972

Jan 9	Buenos Aires 1000 kms	Ferrari 312P	1st
		(with Tim Schenken)	
Jan 23	**ARGENTINE GP**	**March 721**	**6th**
Feb 6	Daytona 24 hours	Ferrari 312P	2nd
		(with Tim Schenken)	
Mar 4	**SOUTH AFRICAN GP**	March 721	**5th**
Mar 12	F2 Mallory Park	March 722	Crashed
Mar 19	F1 Race of Champions	March 721X	12th

RONNIE PETERSON

Date	Event	Car	Result
Mar 25	Sebring 12 hours (with Tim Schenken)	Ferrari 312P	2nd
Mar 30	F1 Interlagos	March 721	2nd
April 1	F2 Thruxton	March 722	1st
April 16	BOAC 1000 kms (with Tim Schenken)	Ferrari 312P	2nd
April 25	Monza 1000 kms (with Tim Schenken)	Ferrari 312P	3rd
May 1	**SPANISH GP**	**March 721X**	**Retired**
May 7	Spa 1000 kms (with Tim Schenken)	Ferrari 312P	Retired
May 14	**MONACO GP**	**March 721X**	**11th**
May 28	Nurburgring 1000 kms (with Tim Schenken)	Ferrari 312P	1st
June 4	**BELGIAN GP**	**March 721X**	**9th**
June 11	F2 Hockenheim	March 722	3rd
June 25	Austrian 1000 kms (with Tim Schenken)	Ferrari 312P	3rd
July 2	**FRENCH GP**	**March 721G**	**5th**
July 15	**BRITISH GP**	**March 721G**	**Crashed**
July 22	Watkins Glen 6 hours (with Tim Schenken)	Ferrari 312P	2nd
July 30	**GERMAN GP**	**March 721G**	**3rd**
Aug 13	**AUSTRIAN GP**	**March 721G**	**12th**
Sept 3	F2 Salzburgring	March 722	Retired
Sept 10	**ITALIAN GP**	**March 721G**	**9th**
Sept 16	F2 Oulton Park	March 722	1st
Sept 24	**CANADIAN GP**	**March 721G**	**Retired**
Oct 1	F2 Hockenheim	March 722	3rd
Oct 8	**UNITED STATES GP**	**March 721G**	**4th**
Oct 22	F1 Brands Hatch	March 721G	Retired
Oct 29	F2 Interlagos	Brabham BT 38	Retired
Nov 5	F2 Interlagos	Brabham BT 38	Retired
Nov 12	F2 Interlagos	Brabham BT 38	Retired

1973

Date	Event	Car	Result
Jan 28	**ARGENTINE GP**	**Lotus 72**	**Retired**
Feb 11	**BRAZILIAN GP**	**Lotus 72**	**Retired**
Mar 3	**SOUTH AFRICAN GP**	**Lotus 72**	**Retired**
Mar 18	F1 Race of Champions	Lotus 72	Retired
April 8	F1 Int Trophy	Lotus 72	2nd
April 29	**SPANISH GP**	**Lotus 72**	**Retired**

May 20	**BELGIAN GP**	**Lotus 72**	**Crashed**
June 3	**MONACO GP**	**Lotus 72**	**3rd**
June 10	F2 Nivelles	Lotus 74	Retired
June 17	**SWEDISH GP**	**Lotus 72**	**2nd**
June 24th	F2 Rouen	Lotus 74	Crashed
July 1	**FRENCH GP**	**Lotus 72**	**1st**
July 14	**BRITISH GP**	**Lotus 72**	**2nd**
July 22	F2 Misano	Lotus 74	Unplaced
July 29	**DUTCH GP**	**Lotus 72**	**Retired**
Aug 5	**GERMAN GP**	**Lotus 72**	**Retired**
Aug 12	F2 Karlskoga	Lotus 74	Unplaced
Aug 19	**AUSTRIAN GP**	**Lotus 72**	**1st**
Aug 26	F2 Enna	Lotus 74	Retired
Sept 9	**ITALIAN GP**	**Lotus 72**	**1st**
Sept 23	**CANADIAN GP**	**Lotus 72**	**Retired**
Oct 7	**UNITED STATES GP**	**Lotus 72**	**1st**
Oct 4	F2 Vallelunga	Lotus 74	Retired

1974

Jan 13	**ARGENTINE GP**	**Lotus 72**	**Retired**
Jan 27	**BRAZILIAN GP**	**Lotus 72**	**6th**
Mar 30	**SOUTH AFRICAN GP**	**Lotus 76**	**Retired**
April 7	F1 Silverstone	Lotus 76	Retired
May 12	**BELGIAN GP**	**Lotus 76**	**Retired**
May 26	**MONACO GP**	**Lotus 72**	**1st**
June 9	**SWEDISH GP**	**Lotus 72**	**Retired**
June 23	**DUTCH GP**	**Lotus 72**	**8th**
July 7	**FRENCH GP**	**Lotus 72**	**1st**
July 20	**BRITISH GP**	**Lotus 72**	**10th**
Aug 4	**GERMAN GP**	**Lotus 76**	**4th**
Aug 11	F2 Karlskoga	March-BMW	1st
Aug 18	**AUSTRIAN GP**	**Lotus 72**	**Retired**
Sept 8	**ITALIAN GP**	**Lotus 72**	**1st**
Sept 22	**CANADIAN GP**	**Lotus 72**	**3rd**
Oct 6	**UNITED STATES GP**	**Lotus 72**	**Retired**

1975

Jan 12	**ARGENTINE GP**	**Lotus 72**	**Retired**
Jan 26	**BRAZILIAN GP**	**Lotus 72**	**15th**
Feb 1/2	Daytona 24 hours	BMW CSL	Retired
Feb 1/2	International Race of Champions final	Chevrolet Camaro	Crashed

Mar 1	SOUTH AFRICAN GP	Lotus 72	10th
Mar 15	F1 Race of Champions	Lotus 72	3rd
Mar 31	F2 Thruxton	March-BMW	Crashed
April 13	F1 Int. Trophy	Lotus 72	Failed to start
April 27	Spanish GP	Lotus 72	Retired
May 11	Monaco GP	Lotus 72	4th
May 25	BELGIAN GP	Lotus 72	Retired
June 8	SWEDISH GP	Lotus 72	9th
June 22	DUTCH GP	Lotus 72	Retired
July 6	FRENCH GP	Lotus 72	10th
July 19	BRITISH GP	Lotus 72	Retired
Aug 3	GERMAN GP	Lotus 72	Retired
Aug 17	AUSTRIAN GP	Lotus 72	5th
Aug 27	Swiss GP, Dijon-Prenois	Lotus 72	4th
Sept 7	ITALIAN GP	Lotus 72	Retired
Oct 5	UNITED STATES GP	Lotus 72	5th

1976

Jan 25	BRAZILIAN GP	Lotus 77	Retired
Mar 6	SOUTH AFRICAN GP	March 761	Crashed
Mar 27	US GP WEST	March 761	10th
May 2	SPANISH GP	March 761	Retired
May 9	Silverstone Six Hours	BMW CSL turbo (with Gunnar Nilsson)	Retired
May 16	BELGIAN GP	March 761	Crashed
May 30	MONACO GP	March 761	Crashed
June 16	SWEDISH GP	March 761	7th
July 4	FRENCH GP	March 761	Retired
July 18	BRITISH GP	March 761	Retired
Aug 1	GERMAN GP	March 761	Crashed
Aug 15	AUSTRIAN GP	March 761	Retired
Aug 29	DUTCH GP	March 761	Retired
Sept 5	Dijon Gp 5	BMW CSL turbo (with Gunnar Nilsson)	Retired
Sept 12	ITALIAN GP	March 761	1st
Oct 3	CANADIAN GP	March 761	9th
Oct 10	UNITED STATES GP	March 761	Retired

1977

Jan 9	ARGENTINE GP	Tyrrell P34	Retired

Jan 23	**BRAZILIAN GP**	**Tyrrell P34**	**Crashed**
Jan 30	Daytona 24 hours	BMW 320i (with David Hobbs and Sam Posey)	Retired
Mar 6	**SOUTH AFRICAN GP**	**Tyrrell P34**	**Retired**
Mar 13	Race of Champions	Tyrrell P34	10th
April 3	**US GP WEST**	**Tyrrell P34**	**Retired**
May 1	Gp 5 Nurburgring	BMW 320i	Retired
May 8	**SPANISH GP**	**Tyrrell P34**	**8th**
May 15	Silverstone Six Hours	BMW 320i (with Helmut Kelleners)	4th
May 22	**MONACO GP**	**Tyrrell P34**	**Retired**
June 5	**BELGIAN GP**	**Tyrrell P34**	**3rd**
June 19	**SWEDISH GP**	**Tyrrell P34**	**Retired**
July 3	**FRENCH GP**	**Tyrrell P34**	**12th**
July 10	Watkins Glen Six Hours	BMW 320 turbo (with David Hobbs)	Crashed
July 31	**GERMAN GP**	**Tyrrell P34**	**9th**
Aug 14	**AUSTRIAN GP**	**Tyrrell P34**	**5th**
Aug 21	Gp 5 Mosport Park	BMW 320 turbo (with David Hobbs)	9th
Aug 28	**DUTCH GP**	**Tyrrell P34**	**Retired**
Sept 11	**ITALIAN GP**	**Tyrrell P34**	**6th**
Sept 26	Brands Hatch Six Hours	BMW 320 turbo (with Hans Stuck)	Crashed
Oct 2	**UNITED STATES GP**	**Tyrrell P34**	**16th**
Oct 9	**CANADIAN GP**	**Tyrrell P34**	**Retired**
Oct 23	**JAPANESE GP**	**Tyrrell P34**	**Retired**

1978

Jan 15	**ARGENTINE GP**	**Lotus 78**	**5th**
Jan 29	**BRAZILIAN GP**	**Lotus 78**	**Crashed**
Mar 4	**SOUTH AFRICAN GP**	**Lotus 78**	**1st**
Mar 19	Silverstone International Trophy	Lotus 78	Crashed
April 2	**US GP WEST**	**Lotus 78**	**4th**
April 30	Gp 5 Nurburgring	BMW 320i	Retired
May 7	**MONACO GP**	**Lotus 78**	**Retired**
May 14	Silverstone Six Hours	BMW 320 turbo (with Hans Stuck)	Retired
May 21	**BELGIAN GP**	**Lotus 78**	**2nd**
May 28	Nurburgring 1000 kms	BMW 320i (with Dieter Quester)	7th

199

RONNIE PETERSON

June 4	SPANISH GP	Lotus 79	2nd
June 18	SWEDISH GP	Lotus 79	3rd
July 2	FRENCH GP	Lotus 79	2nd
July 10	Watkins Glen Six Hours	BMW 320 turbo (with David Hobbs)	Retired
July 16	BRITISH GP	Lotus 79	Retired
July 30	GERMAN GP	Lotus 79	Retired
Aug 13	AUSTRIAN GP	Lotus 79	1st
Aug 27	DUTCH GP	Lotus 79	2nd
Sept 3	Gp 5 Vallelunga	BMW 320 turbo (with Hans Stuck)	Retired
Sept 10	ITALIAN GP	Lotus 78	Crashed, died of injuries.